OECD PROCEEDIN

CENTRE FOR EDUCATIONAL RESEARCH AND

Implementing Inclusive Education

PUBLISHER'S NOTE
The following texts are published in their original form to permit faster distribution at a lower cost.

ORGANISATION FOR ECONOMIC CO-OPERATION AND DEVELOPMENT

ORGANISATION FOR ECONOMIC CO-OPERATION AND DEVELOPMENT

Pursuant to Article 1 of the Convention signed in Paris on 14th December 1960, and which came into force on 30th September 1961, the Organisation for Economic Co-operation and Development (OECD) shall promote policies designed:

- to achieve the highest sustainable economic growth and employment and a rising standard of living in Member countries, while maintaining financial stability, and thus to contribute to the development of the world economy;
- to contribute to sound economic expansion in Member as well as non-member countries in the process of economic development; and
- to contribute to the expansion of world trade on a multilateral, non-discriminatory basis in accordance with international obligations.

The original Member countries of the OECD are Austria, Belgium, Canada, Denmark, France, Germany, Greece, Iceland, Ireland, Italy, Luxembourg, the Netherlands, Norway, Portugal, Spain, Sweden, Switzerland, Turkey, the United Kingdom and the United States. The following countries became Members subsequently through accession at the dates indicated hereafter: Japan (28th April 1964), Finland (28th January 1969), Australia (7th June 1971), New Zealand (29th May 1973), Mexico (18th May 1994), the Czech Republic (21st December 1995), Hungary (7th May 1996), Poland (22nd November 1996) and Korea (12th December 1996). The Commission of the European Communities takes part in the work of the OECD (Article 13 of the OECD Convention).

The Centre for Educational Research and Innovation was created in June 1968 by the Council of the Organisation for Economic Co-operation and Development and all Member countries of the OECD are participants.

The main objectives of the Centre are as follows:

- *analyse and develop research, innovation and key indicators in current and emerging education and learning issues, and their links to other sectors of policy;*
- *explore forward-looking coherent approaches to education and learning in the context of national and international cultural, social and economic change; and*
- *facilitate practical co-operation among Member countries and, where relevant, with non-member countries, in order to seek solutions and exchange views of educational problems of common interest.*

The Centre functions within the Organisation for Economic Co-operation and Development in accordance with the decisions of the Council of the Organisation, under the authority of the Secretary-General. It is supervised by a Governing Board composed of one national expert in its field of competence from each of the countries participating in its programme of work.

Reprinted 1998

FOREWORD

This collection of papers is derived from the dissemination phase of a project, concerned with the integration of children with special educational needs into mainstream schools, undertaken over the period 1990 to 1996 by the Centre for Educational Research and Innovation (CERI) of the OECD.

The first phase of the project had consisted in a series of meetings of researchers and representatives of 21 Member countries of the OECD, followed by the production of individual country reports. The second phase had involved country representatives in monitoring and reporting on 64 case studies undertaken within an agreed common framework. The findings of both phases are detailed in the report *Integrating Students with Special Needs into Mainstream Schools*, published by the OECD in 1995.

This compilation serves as a companion volume to the 1995 publication. Following dissemination conferences in Vaals, the Netherlands in 1993 and in Bethesda, the United States in 1995, participants were invited to adapt their conference presentations for publication purposes, updating them as appropriate. This outcome has been prepared by Don Labon with Peter Evans of the CERI secretariat and is published on the responsibility of the Secretary-General of the OECD.

TABLE OF CONTENTS

Part I. **Background**

Chapter 1. **The OECD Project: integrating students with special needs into mainstream schools**
by Peter Evans and Don Labon

Chapter 2. **Recent developments in OECD Member countries**
by Don Labon and Peter Evans

Part II. **Reform**

Chapter 3. **Quality for all: some comments about inclusive schools from Spanish educational reform**
by Alvaro Marchesi

Chapter 4. **Integration in the Netherlands**
by Cor J.W. Meijer

Chapter 5. **Factors that inclusion must not overlook**

Chapter 6. **How systemic are our systemic reforms?**
by Dianne L. Ferguson

Chapter 7. **What we know about school inclusion**
by Gordon L. Porter

Chapter 8. **The changing roles of school personnel in a restructured and inclusive school**

Chapter 9. **The quality of integration depends on the quality of education for everybody**
by August Dens

Part III. Organisation

Chapter 10. Supporting the classroom teacher in New Brunswick
by Darlene Perner

Chapter 11. Influences of national policies on classroom teaching and curriculum access in England
by Klaus Wedell

Chapter 12. A national strategy for enhancing access to the curriculum in France
by Patrice Couteret

Chapter 13. Pedagogical, curricular and classroom organisation in Italy
by Lucia de Anna

Chapter 14. Integration in the ordinary school in Switzerland
by Gérard Bless

Chapter 15. Inclusion-promoting factors in the Norwegian schools
by Ida Drage

Part IV. **Support**

Chapter 16. **Parental, advisory and administrative support in OECD Countries**
by Don Labon

Chapter 17. **The influence of related services on educational integration in the United States**
by Martha Coutinho and Alan C. Repp

Chapter 18. **Parental, statutory and voluntary support services in Belgium**
by Jean-Jacques Detraux

Chapter 19. **School organisational structures supporting inclusion in Spain**
by Gerardo Echeita

Chapter 20. **The role of special education arrangements in the shift towards less segregation in the Netherlands**
by Aryan van der Leij

Part V. **Accountability and funding**

INTRODUCTION

Over the past 20 years, there have been many changes in our views about the responsibilities that society has towards disabled people, in the ways we expect people with disabilities to respond to education, and in the extent to which we think that they can and should contribute to society. During much of this period, within the OECD, the Centre for Educational Research and Innovation (CERI) has been actively engaged in undertaking research and in considering policy development in this field.

These changes have been given impetus by civil rights movements, by humanitarian concerns and by a better research-based understanding of the educational problems faced by people with disabilities. There is now a widespread belief that policies need to be developed to stimulate the inclusion of children and adults with disabilities in the education systems. Furthermore it is now broadly accepted that school leavers and adults with disabilities should have better access to the labour market.

It is widely recognised that people with disabilities have many skills which could, with appropriate support, be used very effectively in the workplace. The accelerating developments in technology give added force to this conviction and substantial work has been undertaken to identify the kinds of support people with disabilities need at work to enable them to contribute on equal terms with other workers.

These beliefs were endorsed by the Council of the OECD as long ago as 1987, following a high level conference organised by the CERI. The Council considered integration of children with special educational needs within ordinary schools to be the first essential step towards inclusion, and recognised the implications of this for resource allocation, curriculum development and teacher education. The Council also noted that the importance of paid employment for people with disabilities is of growing concern in Member countries of the OECD.

For a person to be in a state of economic dependency or on a very low income because of a disability is contrary to accepted concepts of social justice and of equality of opportunity. Work is more than just a way of making a living. It signifies social recognition and self-affirmation.

The cost to sustain large numbers of citizens in passive dependency can be considerable for countries. It should be noted that the cost of segregated schooling for children with special educational needs is almost always estimated to be more than that of educating them on an inclusive basis.

Including people with disabilities in the regular workplace requires give and take. A mutual understanding has to develop with adjustments being made both by those with and those without disabilities.

In this context, inclusion of children with disabilities in ordinary schools is a particularly important issue. Evidence from Italy, for example, shows that students with disabilities who have been educated in ordinary schools have no wish to work in segregated employment.

The OECD will continue working in this field, with the impetus strengthened by Japan's initiative towards a more caring world. The challenge of inclusive education, and its development in the context of lifelong learning, is great and the problems experienced in achieving it are not easy to solve. Among these is the problem of working out how to use resources most effectively. There are also many problems in the co-ordination of policies and services in such disparate fields as education, health, training, social affairs and the labour market. The papers collected together in this publication provide a wealth of significant insights to help us along the road to success in solving problems of this kind.

Part I

BACKGROUND

CHAPTER 1

THE OECD PROJECT: INTEGRATING STUDENTS WITH SPECIAL NEEDS INTO MAINSTREAM SCHOOLS

by

Peter Evans and Don Labon

Introduction

Since 1978 the Centre for Educational Research and Innovation (CERI) of the OECD has been involved in projects promoting the humanitarian treatment for people with disabilities. The initial project examined the integration of adolescents with disabilities into ordinary secondary schools and the second was concerned with the transition of young people with disabilities from school to work and independent living. The work reported here is that of the third project, which commenced in 1990 under the title "Active Life for Disabled Youth -- Integration in the School". The project consisted of three phases. The first phase focused on identifying current principles and practice with respect to integration in the 21 OECD Member countries that participated, the second phase was concerned with the development of case studies which could provide illustrations of good practice in this field, and the third phase was devoted to the dissemination of findings.

The first phase: country reports

The framework for the first part of the project was established through meetings of CERI staff, consultants with international expertise in this field and representatives of Member countries. The working definition of integration adopted by participants was "that process which maximises the interaction between disabled and non-disabled pupils". Participants then identified the main topics, which included the following:

- countries' policies with respect to integration and the extent to which these policies have been implemented, for example through legislation;

- countries' organisation of education in general and special educational provision in particular;

- statistics concerning the prevalence of special educational needs generally, of particular disabilities, and of types of special educational provision, ranging from help in ordinary classes at one extreme to placement in special schools at the other;

- the nature of the curriculum on offer to children with special educational needs, the extent to which the design of buildings enables them to gain physical access to classrooms, the equipment and special training used to compensate for children's sensory or motor difficulties, the ways in which the curriculum is differentiated to make it suitable for children with a wide range of abilities and interests, and schools' approaches to assessing children's achievements;

- arrangements for the training of teachers, including the presence in initial teacher training courses for all teachers of help in dealing with children's special educational needs, the existence of specialist initial training for those opting to work largely with children with disabilities, the prevalence of and depth of in-service training available to and required of experienced teachers choosing to specialise in this field;

- parental involvement in the assessment of children's requirements for special educational help, in decisions concerning their educational placement, in the management of schools, in providing help in the classroom, in transition to postcompulsory education or employment, and in advocating change at local and national levels; and

- the resourcing of special education, comparative costs of special education in integrated and in segregated settings, and the extent to which different methods of allocation of funds encourage or discourage integration.

On the basis of the agreed framework, country representatives arranged for country reports to be prepared and submitted to the OECD secretariat during the period 1991-92.

The second phase: case studies

The second phase of the project overlapped with the first. In 1991, representatives of the 19 OECD Member countries then participating in the project agreed to gather information, on the basis of a common outline, on one or more case studies per country. The case studies were selected as illustrating good practice conducive to inclusive education within the countries concerned. The schools and other services involved were contributing to the general educational provision within their districts rather than being part of an atypical experimental programme. Central to the framework for the case studies was the concept of a *unit*. A unit was to be a particular innovation, *considered in its context*. The innovation could be, for example, at the level of an individual child, a class, a school, a group of schools, a teacher training programme or a district's support service. The framework for the case studies included the following:

- a description of the functioning of the unit, with reference to its objectives, its management, its duration, its monitoring, its financial support, its relationship with other services, and the extent to which it enhanced integration;

- an evaluation of the work of the unit, particularly with respect to the curriculum it offered, the socialisation experiences it provided for students with disabilities, its association with support services, and the extent to which associated health, education and social services were integrated with one another; and

- answers to core questions concerning the programme's initiation, steps taken to avoid potential problems, difficulties encountered and solutions found, any obstacles remaining, insights obtained as a result of the programme's implementation, and reactions of people outside the programme to the results it achieved.

In all cases information concerning a unit was gathered through perusal of relevant documentation. In most cases this was followed up through discussion with people already familiar with the development, either through their being involved directly in the activities or through their having advised on, organised, supervised or monitored programmes. Questionnaires were used in some cases. Much of the discussion occurred within the context of on-site visits. In some cases, discussions took place with children and with their parents as well as with professionals. Most visits involved informal and participant observation of integration work.

Altogether, 64 case studies were undertaken and the reports arising from them were completed in 1993. Nineteen of the units were at the level of an individual or a classroom, sixteen focused on a single school, fifteen were concerned with a group of schools, four with support services external to schools, and ten with training programmes.

Findings

Syntheses of the individual country reports and case study reports were completed during 1993 and written reports of the composite findings were fed back to the OECD secretariat and to the project's consultants and country representatives in time for the start of the dissemination phase, which commenced in late 1993. The composite findings were published by the OECD as a single volume, under the title *Integrating Students with Special Needs into Mainstream Schools*, in 1995.

Findings arising from the country reports

The compilation arising from the country reports includes a presentation of the most extensive set of statistics on the prevalence of children with special educational needs and the educational provision made for them in OECD member countries to date. Comparison of data across countries was made difficult by variations in terminology, and there was clearly a need for international agreement on an educationally based classification system. The statistics showed marked differences across countries in the extent to which different disabilities were recognised and provided for.

Former emphasis on medical classification of children with disabilities had given way to the dominant belief that, if their special educational needs are met appropriately, their development can accelerate and many of them can lead productive and relatively normal lives. There was substantial support for the view that many of the children educated in separate special schools could and should benefit, along with the broader group of children with special needs, by attending ordinary schools. Government policies across OECD countries by this time favoured increased integration and, with the principle agreed, the emphasis had shifted to determining the most effective means of achieving this in practice.

In many schools, opportunities for integration were enhanced through the flexible organisation of ordinary classes and through the deployment of within-class support teachers. Full integration is precluded if classes are streamed according to ability, though this can help some children transfer from special schools to ordinary schools, or if a proportion failing to reach a designated standard by the end of a school year have to repeat the same work by remaining in the same class for a further year. The academic and pre-vocational requirements of secondary schools presented significant problems for full integration, though many of these problems appeared surmountable. Promising features of several countries' developments included resource centres in ordinary schools and co-operation across schools.

Some schools offered a standard curriculum to all, some provided separate courses for those with special needs, and some provided a curriculum that was differentiated sufficiently to enable children of different abilities to work individually or in groups on similar tasks at their own levels in the same classroom. This third approach, that of within-class curriculum differentiation, while common in only a few OECD countries as yet, was gaining ground generally and was the only one seen to sustain extensive integration. To be effective it requires endorsement at national, regional and local policy levels, flexible support services, formative assessment linked with teaching, and high levels of skill among class teachers.

Because teaching children of varying abilities is complex, there is an overwhelming case in favour of making some training for teaching these children an intrinsic part of initial training for all teachers. As many serving teachers do not have the attitudes, skills and understanding that effective integration requires, in-service training also has a key role to play in any moves towards integration. Furthermore, advanced training is required by those specialising in this field. While examples of all three modes of training were reported, there appeared to be much room for further development of each, and for evaluation of their effectiveness.

Across OECD countries, parental involvement had undoubtedly been a driving force in the development of special education. With regard to the majority of children with special needs, the force was in favour of integration. Parents' rights to be treated as partners in the assessment and educational placement of their children were recognised in some countries, though in practice professionals did not always ensure that these rights were respected. There were welcome signs, however, of parents' increasing participation in the day to day work of schools.

While comparative costs of integrated and segregated special education are extremely difficult to estimate, such evidence as there was indicated that, for the vast majority of children with special needs, education in integrated settings was not inordinately costly and was in any case less expensive than their placement in special schools. Some methods of allocating funding were found to be more conducive to integration than others.

The main body of the report ends with an outline of key features which any integration plan, whether it is at the level of a country, a region or a district, can usefully exhibit. These features are presented in terms of identification, consultation, assessment of existing strengths, target setting, implementation, evaluation and resourcing. The report's appendix consists of brief accounts, on a country by country basis, of policies, legislation and population statistics relating to special educational needs.

Findings arising from the case studies

The bulk of the report consists of presentation of selected case studies, clustered in accordance with size of unit, starting with the smallest. Initial presentations focus on the individual classroom, looking at ways in which teaching can be adapted to meet special educational needs. Strategies used by teachers included teaching only selected aspects of the mainstream curriculum, using technological devices to ensure that children had access to ordinary learning materials, providing extra teaching help, introducing alternative curriculum content, and arranging periodic withdrawal from the ordinary classroom for individual or small group work.

While these teaching strategies provided academic benefits for children with special needs, and while there were also social gains for teachers and for ordinary children, one of the more disconcerting findings of the studies was that children with special needs were often socially isolated. Some of the studies referred to means through which this isolation could be reduced.

It is not until these strategies are placed in the context of schools as a whole that the overall shape of integration developments begins to emerge. Examples of schools' integration programmes provided the bases for a series of statements concerning conditions which had been seen to facilitate the implementation of successful whole school policies. These included wholehearted promotion and evaluation of programmes, flexible organisation of classes, individual and group programmes at various levels, programmes to develop social as well as academic skills, support staff with general credibility as well as special needs expertise, and arrangements giving staff time to consult and plan as well as to teach.

Ways in which integration arrangements in schools can be influenced by factors outside the ordinary school are considered. These include the contributions of parents and other members of the community, and outreach work through which staff of special schools are playing an increasing part in assisting the progressive integration into ordinary schools of children who in former times might have been educated in special schools. In-service training was seen to have a crucial part to play in facilitating integration. Staff running such training could be based in ordinary schools, special schools, external support services or teacher training establishments, with each group having particular kinds of contribution to make.

The report then presents an account of the problems which were found in the case studies to present obstacles to integration, distinguishing between those characteristic of the processes of initiation, implementation, maintenance and evaluation, and considers possible solutions. The final chapter of the body of the report takes account of the country reports contributing to the first phase of the project as well as of the case study reports prepared for the second phase. It summarises, through a series of brief statements, what appear to be the main features of good practice in inclusive education. Appended to the report are summaries, on a country by country basis, of the 64 studies undertaken in the 19 participating countries.

The third phase: dissemination

By late 1993 the written reports presenting composite findings from the first two phases of the project had been distributed to country representatives, putting them in a position to disseminate these findings within their own countries. In addition, two international conferences had been planned, one to be located in Europe and one in America. The first took place in Vaals, the Netherlands, in December 1993 and the second in Bethesda, Maryland, the United States, in June 1995, shortly after the OECD's formal publication of the volume detailing the findings arising from the project's first two phases. People invited to the conferences included the project's participants, others with international expertise in the field of special education, academics, administrators, practitioners in special education, other professionals concerned with disability, and representatives of voluntary bodies and parent groups. Total attendance exceeded 200.

The present publication serves as a companion volume to the 1995 publication. It consists of two background papers, this one and a paper providing brief update information on events in participating countries subsequent to their production of country reports on developments up to 1992, followed by 23 papers arising from the two dissemination conferences. Following the dissemination conferences, participants were invited to adapt their conference presentations for publication purposes, updating them as appropriate.

The conference papers have been grouped, according to four dominant themes, under the headings of reform, organisation, support and funding. In fact most of the papers touch on more than one theme and some contain information of relevance to all four, so inter-related are the issues in this field, but the loose classification adopted here is intended to reflect the main thrust of each and so be of help to the reader.

The seven papers clustered under the heading of **reform** are all concerned with inclusive education for children with special educational needs as part of a broader platform for reform, both in the education system as a whole and in society more generally, in family life for example and in the world of work. Issues considered include problems experienced at government level in implementing reform, the importance of recognising social factors as intrinsic to educational reform and not just providing a context for it, and the need for fairly fundamental changes in participants' perceptions both of children's and of teachers' roles if the reforms necessary to inclusive education are to be lasting.

The second theme is that of **organisation**. The six papers clustered here illustrate various effects, not all beneficial as far as inclusive education is concerned, of organisation at different levels: at the level of a national curriculum, of national resource centres, of regional groups with similar professional interests, of a district-wide system for providing both within-school and outside-school help for teachers, of teachers' in-class decision-making strategies, and of individual assessment leading to a teaching programme and evaluation of progress.

The concept of **support**, providing the theme for the third cluster, is explored through a further six papers, which among them consider the kinds of educational support that can be provided by parents and by administrators as well as through the advice offered by professional support services external to the schools. Multi-disciplinary co-operation is stressed, contributions of voluntary organisations are described, the relative merits of within-school and outside-school support systems are compared, and the contributions that the staff of special schools can make to inclusive education are considered.

The fourth cluster, presented under the title of accountability **funding**, tackles some of the most vexed questions relevant to inclusive education. Several papers included in other clusters have already referred to problems concerning accountability funding and the four papers included here take the debate further. They illustrate the complexity of these issues, analyse attempts to assess the extent of needs for extra resources, and look at ways of modifying systems that, perhaps inadvertently, promote segregation. The final paper, focuses on regional variations in assessment and, highlights difficulties that can be encountered at national level in identifying and reporting children's special needs and, inevitably, the extent to which their calls on funding are justified.

While this publication constitutes the final formal product of the OECD's "integration in the school" project, it is hoped that both this and the 1995 publication will continue to provide useful reference sources for people working in this field during the next few years. They are designed primarily to enable government ministers to review the implementation of the integration policies in their own countries, within an international context. Both, however, include information likely to be of interest to teachers, other professionals concerned with special educational needs, and families in which there is a child with a disability.

CHAPTER 2

RECENT DEVELOPMENTS IN OECD MEMBER COUNTRIES

by

Don Labon and Peter Evans

Introduction

This paper summarises some recent developments in inclusive education. It follows on from the publication *Integrating Students with Special Needs into Mainstream Schools* (OECD, 1995), which reports findings of the first two phases of a project undertaken by the OECD's Centre for Educational Research and Innovation over the period 1990 to 1996 and involving 21 Member countries.

The first part of the publication, reflecting the first phase of the project, draws on country reports submitted in 1992 and summarises developments in special education principles, practice and prospects across Member countries, considering in particular their practice in educating children with special educational needs in ordinary schools. The second part summarises findings of the second phase of the project, which involved Member countries in providing case studies reporting examples of good practice. The third phase of the project consists of disseminating findings.

The database for the present paper consists of accounts, provided by representatives of 19 Member countries, of developments since 1992. The section headings used here echo the chapter headings of the first part of the 1995 publication and within each section the information is presented largely on a country by country basis. This should help the reader to follow up developments in two ways: firstly in terms of the main issues presented in the 1995 publication, and secondly from the baseline of the data encapsulated in the 1995 publication's summaries of individual countries' reports and case studies.

Policy and legislation

In all the countries providing reports declared policies continue to support the inclusive education of students with disabilities.

In Australia inclusive education at school and post-school levels has been enhanced through the implementation of the 1992 Disability Discrimination Act, the 1993 National Equity Program for Schools and the 1994 Working Nation initiative. The goal is increasing but not total inclusion and the emphasis is on increased educational performance rather than on integration as an end in itself.

The 1993 amendment to the Austrian Federal School Act extended the aims and objectives of elementary education to include the concept of social integration. In order to implement this, the scope of elementary schools has been increased, and they can now apply a special school curriculum in suitable cases. Earlier terminology relating to particular disabilities has now been replaced by the more general concept of special educational needs.

The emphasis of current policy in Belgium is on enhancing facilities for differentiation in elementary schools, in an attempt to reduce placement in special schools. Existing regulations have been amended to provide support for children with disabilities in ordinary schools, with support for one year by special school staff for those returning from special schools, but this support is not extended to children with severe learning difficulties.

Denmark's 1994 Education Act, while retaining responsibility for identifying the general aims of teaching and for drawing up curriculum guidelines, passes on to teachers and pupils the responsibility of together identifying the objectives which individual pupils will try to achieve.

In France, since the passing of the Education Law in 1989, local authorities have been under obligation to educate all children with disabilities. Amendments in 1991, provided for some of them to be integrated into ordinary schools with the target of obtaining the school leaving diploma, the CAP.

German legislation recognises the rights of children with disabilities to education in ordinary schools, with parents having the responsibility of deciding whether these rights are to be exercised. Guidelines promoting inclusive education now exist in all 16 Länder.

Legislation on compulsory education passed in Iceland in 1995 re-affirms concern for children with special needs, by avoiding mention of special education as such and by emphasising that each pupil is to receive the education best suited to that child's ability.

Italian legislation of 1992, reinforced by presidential decree in 1994, stated criteria for the certification of children with disabilities, established procedures leading to individual education plans, and strengthened existing interdisciplinary links.

While ordinary schools and special schools are still subject to separate legislation in the Netherlands, the passing of a single law covering special education in both settings is under consideration. The special schools involved are those for children with mild to moderate behavioural or learning difficulties, and the proposed legislation also takes account of very young children at risk.

The re-evaluation of special education in Norway, started in 1991 and involving five ministries, is due for completion, with a white paper to be issued in time for Parliament to consider its recommendations in 1997. One consideration will be improving the co-ordination of existing services to enable users to have easier access to them.

In Spain, legislation planned for implementation from 1995 is expected to establish the concept of special educational needs, thus broadening concern with disability to include all students who need extra help or curriculum adaptation. The intention is that it will also cover children with social disadvantage and gifted children. It includes consideration of placement and review procedures, curriculum adaptation and parental rights and duties.

In the interests of inclusiveness, Swedish legislation currently carries no reference to special education.

Part lll of the United Kingdom's Education Act 1993 builds upon the special education arrangements prescribed in the 1981 Education Act. It sets statutory time limits for completing statements concerning children's special educational needs; it requires ordinary schools to publish their policies for special needs; it gives parents disagreeing with proposed arrangements for meeting special needs the right of appeal to an independent tribunal; it requires schools and local authorities to have regard to a code of practice, published in 1994.

In the United States, re-authorisation of the 1990 Individuals with Disabilities Education Act (IDEA) includes consideration of the allocation of funds for research into the evaluation of children's progress and for the training of teachers. It is likely to shift the emphasis of accountability to include measures of outcomes as well as of processes. This is mainly because at present, with much variation from one state to another, about half the children with disabilities in the country are not included in the assessment systems used.

Educational organisation

Reports from Australia, Germany, Greece, Iceland, Norway, Spain, Turkey, the United Kingdom and the United States all indicate continuing increases in the proportion of students with disabilities educated in ordinary schools. There are also indications of increasing numbers of students with disabilities receiving post-compulsory education.

In Australia the main trend over the period has been towards the enrolment of students with mild to moderate learning disabilities in special classes or units attached to ordinary schools rather than in special schools.

The number of children recognised as having special educational needs in Austria has increased, though the number placed in special schools has remained constant . At regional level, certain special schools are to function as resource centres, supporting elementary schools and keeping them informed. In the existing pilot study of inclusive education, integrated classes are organised on the basis of classes of 20 including four children with disabilities and taught by two teachers, one of them specialising in special education. The pilot study is to continue until 1997.

In Belgium the policy of enhancing differentiation is being supported by the provision of extra teachers for young children in ordinary schools and nursery classes, with continuation of this provision being dependent on its being used effectively.

Following the lead taken internationally by the Department of Education of the New Brunswick province of Canada in the development of inclusive education, over 1993 and 1994 the student services administrators for the school districts sought to consolidate progress through the production of a document, "Best Practices for Inclusion", issued in 1994. The document affirms principles and presents features of best practice at district, school, classroom and community levels. During 1995 it was used by districts to evaluate the implementation of their plans for inclusive education in their schools.

In Denmark compulsory education continues to be managed nationally through a cross-ministerial committee for children. Only about one per cent of the school population are assessed as requiring extensive special education but among these the fraction placed in special classes has increased over the past decade, from a quarter to a third. While educational opportunities have been continuing to improve progressively for the vast majority of children, this has not been the case for some 15 per cent whose increasing difficulties are due primarily to increasing social disadvantage, exacerbated by unemployment, rather than to intrinsic disability.

There has been much development in higher education in France, with a co-ordinator appointed for students with disabilities in universities. Information is published about the types of course available to students with disabilities and about funding opportunities, for example to enable students with physical disabilities to have secretarial help in writing their theses. Over recent years there has been a 20 per cent increase in the number of students with disabilities entering universities. Despite the publicity, however, some universities are still lagging behind in providing facilities.

In Germany, the proportion of the school population attending special schools is now down to 3.3 per cent. Change has been enhanced by the recommendations in 1994 of the Standing Conference of the Ministers of Education and Cultural Affairs of the Länder, that children who have disabilities and are of elementary school age are expected to enrol in ordinary schools on an integrated basis. Some 150 schools are involved in an experimental inclusive education programme. Developments include implementation of a model whereby a class of 20 children including two with disabilities has a full-time teacher plus a support teacher for eight periods a week, with one of the two specialising in special education if possible.

Developments in Greece have been helped by examples of good practice stemming from the European Union's HELIOS II programme and by a national decree in 1993 concerning the development of teaching support in ordinary elementary and secondary schools. The number of students with disabilities helped through teaching support in ordinary schools increased by 15 per cent over the two year period 1993 to 1994.

Responsibility for the running of compulsory schools in Iceland has shifted from the state to the municipalities.

A commission established in Ireland in 1991 to review special education reported in 1993, recommending that, except in very exceptional circumstances, special education should take place in ordinary schools. The report also recommended that with respect to children with disabilities a co-ordinating committee for health and education be established, and this is now in place. A white paper proposing the management of education through 20 regional boards has been issued.

With inclusive education policies and practice having been established in Italy since the 1970's, by 1993 99.9 per cent of children of compulsory school age in the state system were attending ordinary schools. Some two per cent had been formally assessed as having disabilities and as a result were receiving specialist teaching support, mainly within ordinary classes.

Since 1991, there has been a project running in the Netherlands whereby co-operation between ordinary schools and special schools for children with mild to moderate behavioural or learning difficulties takes the form of regional networks. The aim is that in these networks the special schools will provide support to ordinary schools in the form of advice to teachers and through special classes. The country still has 3.8 per cent of children attending these special schools. In 1995, the mid-term review of the project concluded that it was not yet sufficiently successful to be put into practice more generally. In 1996 it was agreed that schools for children with different kinds of learning difficulty will be amalgamated to function as more generalised special schools.

From 1997 compulsory education in Norway, currently starting at age seven, will run from age six, lasting therefore for ten years. More special schools have closed, there are now very few institutions for children with severe learning disabilities, and the competence centres have developed their services further. The national centres continue to provide for the rarer and more severe disabilities and the regional centres for milder difficulties, with each centre having its own steering group. At upper secondary level (age 16 to 19) there has been a drive in recent years to increase inclusive education for students with disabilities. Although most are in ordinary settings, there is still more segregation here than in primary schools, with some 30 per cent still in special classes, and special schools for the deaf continue to exist. There is much variation both across schools and within schools; for example, there is more inclusive education in vocational courses than in academic courses.

In Spain, most students with disabilities now attend ordinary schools, with special schools used only for those with more severe or complex disabilities, and with links between ordinary and special schools being strengthened. Secondary schools receive extra help in providing for students with special needs and the students' progress is being monitored centrally. In some of the schools with students with hearing impairment, sign language interpreters are provided.

Since 1990 special education in Sweden has been decentralised to the extent that the municipalities have full responsibility for virtually all state education. The municipalities themselves are decentralising to some extent, by devolving responsibilities down to district level. The state continues to provide advisers, some resource centres and some special schooling for the deaf, but is seeking to pass the education of the deaf to the municipalities as well.

Pilot studies in 91 schools in Turkey have been undertaken as a means of promoting the integration of children with special needs at pre-school, primary and secondary phases of education. Provision is supported through in-service training, through consideration of architectural arrangements, and through the development of teaching materials.

In the United States, all states have systems for inclusion, with particular attention paid to the needs of those with severe learning difficulties. As more children with disabilities are being included in ordinary school programmes, the strains on the system are beginning to show and there continues to be a need to counter resistance to these developments. Under the leadership of the Department of Education, the Goals 2000 programme now involves goal setting for all children, not just for those with disabilities. Developments in inclusion practices are generating needs for teacher training programmes to help teachers to work in multi-disciplinary teams.

Curriculum

In Australia a national curriculum framework was introduced in 1994, and this has led to consideration of ways in which curriculum content can be taught and progress assessed without these processes being to the disadvantage of students with disabilities. A likely result is that students with disabilities will have access to a broader curriculum than that which has traditionally been taught in special schools. Within the national framework, individual educational programmes are being developed for students with disabilities, with those approaching school leaving age having transition plans to help them prepare for work or for post-compulsory education.

In New Brunswick, Canada, there is an emphasis on developing a smooth transition from the curriculum at one age level to that at the next. This progresses from more exploratory activities in the early years, through an integrated curriculum with strong family connections in the middle years to a range of academic and practical activities in the high schools. Within this framework, and given the use of multi-level teaching methods, most students with disabilities are able to manage without the need for special courses, which are now being phased out.

Under the 1994 Education Act, in Denmark the curriculum for individual children with special needs can be modified with respect to the range of subjects followed, the number of lessons taken weekly, and the arrangements for assessment of educational achievement.

In Germany, teachers in the Länder joining the country on unification are still having to adjust to a new curriculum and for some this adjustment is overwhelming to the extent that it leaves them with little time to relate constructively to social problems. While the attitudes of teachers in ordinary schools generally are not always in favour of inclusive education, some improvements in attitude are being stimulated through increasing co-operation with staff of special schools and through pre-school programmes for children with disabilities. In some Länder, steps are being taken to improve vocational training and job prospects more generally for young people with special educational needs.

The Icelandic Ministry of Education is planning to introduce a new national curriculum, covering both compulsory education and post-compulsory further education.

The more generalised special schools to be developed in the Netherlands will offer the same curriculum as do primary schools.

In Spain, written guidelines have been issued to help teachers adapt the National Curriculum to meet special educational needs. Some of the materials developed are designed for use in teaching students with severe learning difficulties.

Parental and community involvement

In Australia, a Commonwealth-funded project concerned with good practice in inclusive education, completed in 1992, stressed the importance of empowering parents to be partners in educational decision-making and of having parents and other members of the community sit on key committees concerned with funding for special education.

The Department of Education in New Brunswick has appointed a consultant responsible for promoting parental involvement in their children's education. Programmes on paired reading and on motivating children have been developed and there have been multi-media presentations across the province.

Parents generally in Denmark are increasingly demanding of quality in education. In the area of special educational needs they are seeking more precise diagnosis, and increases in recent years in the number of placements of children in special classes are partly in response to parents' wishes.

Local authorities in France are to publicise their schools' facilities for pupils with disabilities, so that parents are aware of what is available.

Since unification Germany has seen improvements in parental and community involvement in education, particularly in the new Länder. Among parents of ordinary children, however, there are still concerns that the education of their children might be slowed down by the presence of children with disabilities, and because of this particular care has to be taken in developing inclusive education programmes.

Parents of children with disabilities in Greece are showing increasing interest in obtaining teaching support for their children, and are co-operating with teachers in ordinary schools to secure this.

In Iceland there is a strengthening both of parental organisations concerned with their children's disabilities and of organisations run by people who themselves have disabilities.

As part of the proposed arrangements for reducing special school placements in the Netherlands, a permanent committee for child care will advise on placement of children in primary or special schools and parental involvement in decisions concerning placement will be strengthened.

Videotapes have been developed in Spain for use by staff of support services in helping parents of young children with communication problems, including those arising from hearing impairment.

Parents in Sweden are pressing for inclusive education of better quality for children with disabilities, and the government is seeking to strengthen their currently limited involvement in the work of schools, but schools may well resist this.

Support services

In Australia, as part of the 1993 National Equity Program for Schools, supplementary funding has been provided to help in the development of support services such as those provided by peripatetic teachers and by school transition officers, who help students with disabilities plan for life after school. Voluntary organisations concerned with particular disabilities have been especially influential in the development of support services.

While there are no longer any special schools in New Brunswick, there are some families whose children with sensory impairment receive residential education in another province. As inclusive education proceeds the need for residential education is diminishing and the number of such places is planned to be down to 10 or fewer by 1996.

The French now have a system of early warning of disability, organised on a multi-disciplinary basis.

In Germany, multi-disciplinary resource centres which may be based in ordinary or special schools provide support services for children with disabilities, and for children at risk more generally, from pre-school level upwards. They undertake assessment, give advice and make recommendations concerning educational placement. As part of a new service network, they seek to integrate the work of staff of education, health and welfare services, and to liaise with voluntary organisations. One aim is to develop shared responsibility among the various groups with which they are concerned.

There is continuing growth in Spain in the number of people employed in support services concerned with students with disabilities, particularly those at secondary school level.

Training

In Australia, as more students with disabilities are taught in ordinary schools, work with them is receiving increasing emphasis, both in initial teacher training and in in-service programmes.

Teacher training establishments in Austria are now obliged to train teachers to teach integrated classes. Within the integration programme there is no longer an extra allowance for special education teaching, and this is having an adverse effect on take-up of training places for special education.

In New Brunswick, all students on initial teacher training courses take a one term course in special education, choosing from a range of options concerned with the inclusive education of either children or adults. In Canada as a whole, a national in-service training programme for teachers, designed to maximise the participation of children with physical disabilities in physical education programmes, was introduced in 1994. In addition to the implementation of this particular programme, the emphasis in the New Brunswick province, both at district level and within individual schools, is on multi-level teaching and on fostering active and co-operative learning.

Recent increases in inclusive education in Greece have been accompanied by increases in related training for teachers. The number of teachers attending two year courses in special education almost doubled during the 1993-94 period.

Norway's teacher training for special education, which attracts teachers from many countries, has now shifted from its college base and has been incorporated into the university system. Being sited within the university campus should enhance the institute's prospects for developing its research activities.

In Spain, in-service training in special education offered to teachers through a network of teachers' centres now includes a scheme concerned with new technologies. Because developments in inclusive education require developments in the curriculum generally and not just in special education, in 1994 the country's national resource centre for special education became integrated within a new centre concerned with curriculum development for all students.

Resources

In Australia, the fact that developments in inclusive education have been found to be cost-effective has enabled education authorities to divert some of the funding for special education into work with young children and with students with severe disabilities.

Funding for schools in Austria comes from various sources: different groups raise funds for school buildings, the salaries of special education teachers (some 4 000 in special schools and some 2 000 in integrated settings) are met by the Ministry of Education, teacher training is supported at Federal level, and resources such as books are paid for by the Ministry of Finance and Family Affairs.

The funding of extensive special education in Denmark is gradually being devolved from county level to municipal level.

In Germany, the funding of inclusive education has increased in recent years. Students with disabilities are provided with extra financial support. Technical equipment needed by students with disabilities in ordinary or special schools is often provided by welfare services.

It continues to be the case in the Netherlands that children in special schools receive extra funding. Those with special needs in ordinary schools receive some extra funding under strict conditions. The arrangement is being reviewed at government level and a white paper on pupil-based financing is in preparation, with a view to implementing new legislation from 1998. With the goal of reducing segregated education from its present 3.8 per cent to 2 per cent, special schools will receive budgets for 2 per cent only, with the money for the other 1.8 per cent going to primary schools. The same process is being started at secondary level.

In Sweden the state pays for any help to meet a child's special needs in the ordinary school beyond that of 20 extra teaching hours a week. This arrangement is in need of revision, as it encourages schools to over-provide and municipalities to seek unnecessary subsidies.

Federal disability insurance in Switzerland is being revised which should more easily allow for children with disabilities to be educated in ordinary classes. Currently it only applies if they are in special classes, and this serves to discourage inclusive education.

The code of practice published in 1994 in the United Kingdom had been developed by the Department for Education in partnership with government health and social services agencies and in consultation with local authorities. Implementation of this and other special education developments arising from the Education Act 1993 is funded through a programme which grants money to help schools develop their policies for special educational needs, to help local education authorities to develop parent partnership schemes, and to help in the training of teachers.

In the United States, re-authorisation of the 1990 Individuals with Disabilities Education Act is likely to carry the requirement that state funding systems are neutral with respect to integration or segregation.

Part II

REFORM

CHAPTER 3

QUALITY FOR ALL: SOME COMMENTS ABOUT INCLUSIVE SCHOOLS FROM SPANISH EDUCATIONAL REFORM

by

Alvaro Marchesi

Introduction

This paper is organised on the basis of experiences in the Spanish education reform and in the integration project started ten years ago. Three general conclusions could be underlined.

- The first, and perhaps the most important, is that the education of children with special educational needs and the changes required may not be undertaken to the full if, at the same time, the necessary changes to the whole education system are not made. It is the whole education system, and not just one aspect which should be reformed to make inclusive education possible.

- The second conclusion to be emphasised is that integration requires a new perspective in the school, which is sensitive to the specific demands on each and every one of the students. Inclusive education is not only the responsibility of those teachers who are more committed to all their students. It has to be a responsibility of the school as a whole, which has to rethink its educational aims, its organisation, its assessment system and its methodology to provide for children with special educational needs.

- The third conclusion is that it is necessary to be sensitive to changes in society and to adapt the education system as quickly as possible to them. If not, we run the risk of being out of date, maintaining attractive ideas but without any real influence. New economic and social situations are evolving; rises in unemployment, greater competition in finding jobs, the growing demands on the education system, which may not always be homogeneous, the greater presence of different cultures in our society and in schools, the increase in racist and xenophobic movements, the increase in pluralism, changes in value, in the conception of human relationships and social organisations.

At the same time, however, people are demanding more quality in schools and choose those which better respond to their interests. The question now is: what must the education authorities do in order to improve inclusive schools so that they are chosen by a growing number of parents?

Besides these general conclusions, it is possible, from the experience of the Spanish educational reform, to reveal the three most determinant factors which influence schools to be open to all and to be of high quality: teachers' professional development, schools' organisational improvement and educational authorities' commitment to inclusive schools. Let me present you with some comments about them.

Teachers' professional development

The education of children with special needs in ordinary schools demands a commitment for all teachers. It is no simple task to provide educational attention to these students and this cannot be based solely on the good-will of a few isolated teachers. Participation and efforts from the whole educational community are required. The importance of team work and school organisation to the service of a specific project will be commented upon in more detail later. What is important now is to emphasise that team work, the possibility for a school to effectively develop its own autonomy, is based on participation from teachers. The teachers, both individually and as a whole, are a fundamental factor for guaranteeing the quality of an integration project.

If the role of teachers is so important, one needs to analyse the conditions which would effectively facilitate the incorporation of these children into education. These conditions may rapidly be defined in two words: interest and competence. By "interest" I refer to teachers' attitudes, to their theories about the education of children with special needs and their willingness to participate in teaching those children. "Competence" refers to the possibilities a teacher has to successfully meet the demands of these children to train them, and to have the means available in order to do so. Both terms are closely linked. The initial positive attitude towards integration may change as difficulties arise in putting it into practice. And the reverse. A positive experience in daily work with children who have learning disabilities leads to decreasingly negative attitudes.

Teachers' attitudes are also closely linked with professional satisfaction and professional perspective. Integration requires greater effort from teachers. Only those teachers who consider that special educational needs teaching enters within their professional responsibilities, and who are relatively satisfied with their professional lives, will seriously undertake this task happily and consistently.

Professional satisfaction of teachers is thus a very important factor for encouraging integration. There is no doubt that basic and rapid professional satisfaction of teaching staff depends on the conditions of work and pay. However, it would be too limiting to equate professional satisfaction with remuneration. There are other elements, perhaps not sufficiently appreciated, which could greatly contribute to improving the professional satisfaction of the teacher: greater human resources and materials in the school, fewer children in the class, greater support and training facilities, greater special appreciation, professional promotion. In this way, special appreciation for working with children who have special needs, expressed in terms of professional promotion, could be the stimulus needed and a way of attributing greater value to those activities which demand more effort and preparation. It is thus possible to progressively change teachers' attitudes towards integration through professional stimuli and positive experiences.

If "interest" is a necessary condition to efficiently integrate children with special needs, "competence" is a sufficient condition to achieve it. How does a teacher feel sufficiently competent to resolve the problems posed for educating these students? Mainly, by having obtained suitable training and being aware that permanent training is guaranteed, by knowing that specialised help is on hand when necessary, and by being able to deploy the right human and material resources to undertake the work.

36

Initial and continued training of teachers are the priority aims for guaranteeing educational quality. This training must take into consideration the professional profile demanded of the teacher at the present moment in time: the ability to make decisions about the curriculum work in a team, understand cultural and generational changes, and diversify methods to attend to all the different needs of the students.

Schools' organisational improvement

A school is not just the sum of each one of its teachers, going about their jobs in an individual, autonomous way. The school is an institution with its own aims and rules, with communication systems, specific participation and management, related to other organisations or institutions in its environment, and with its own way of managing resources. A school may have all these elements -- aims, rules, participation, management, relationships, financial managements all well established, to the service of a common, revised and periodically up-dated project. Or, on the other hand, it may leave these elements unclear, leaving it up to the dynamics of individuals to form rules. The first option seems clearly the most appropriate to give all students access to the curriculum.

The education of children with special needs requires a clearer definition of educational aims, of the necessary curricular adaptations, and of the systems of assessment and promotion to be used in conjunction with them. Moreover, educational attention to these children requires greater co-ordination among teachers who work with them, in their methods, in the expectations they have and in the ways in which they make use of the available resources. Perhaps the education of children with no learning difficulties could be undertaken without any good organisational development existing within the school. But for the children with special education needs this is very difficult. It can therefore be clearly confirmed that a whole school approach could be particularly important for improving educational progress of children with special needs. Evidence exists from educational research that supports this fact, confirming that those with the greatest learning difficulties can be more significantly affected by the overall school quality than can those students who are more advanced.

The existence of an individual educational project, created by the teachers themselves, expresses the willingness of a school to put this whole school approach into practice. Assessment carried out in Spain on the integration of students with special needs confirmed its importance. The presence of an educational project in the school was the most important factor for differentiating between schools and evaluating results. The educational project also reflected a positive predisposition from teachers towards integration and progress in communication and co-ordination.

Analysis of the different projects revealed that, although their existence was good from the start, it was also necessary to consider their quality. A good project is one which covers the educational needs of all students and includes co-ordination among teachers, revision of work, and adaptation of the school's results. The most important conditions for producing a good educational project were the following:

1. cohesion of the teacher team and basic agreement about the concept of integration;

2. positive attitudes towards integration;

3. efficiency and flexibility in organising the school; and

4. training of teachers to respond to educational changes put forward by integration.

In previous paragraphs reference has already been made to teacher training and attitudes. It must be emphasised that the organisational development of the school is one of the strongest strategies, not only for making an educational project possible but also for being able to meet the needs of all students with the curriculum.

The conception of the curriculum as a process of decision-making, by a team of teachers wishing to guarantee a suitable education for all students, necessitates a well organised school in order for decisions to be taken easily and with the right participation. Education must be understood to be a continuous process of problem solving. Schools must therefore be co-operative organisations which are capable of finding the right solutions.

School organisation should be established with this aim: to allow teachers to develop the curriculum in a co-operative manner, through a common project in which the whole educational community is involved. It is therefore necessary to appreciate the type of organisation existing in each school, to discover what type of participation is present, what problems teachers are trying to solve and how they go about adopting decisions.

The role of the head teacher is fundamental to this process and should be defined mainly for ability to create participatory organisations which find solutions to all problems posed. Participation is, in turn, only possible when an atmosphere of mutual appreciation exists, when different members of the educational community support one another and when their educational aims are shared.

The organisational development of a school is not an aim which can be achieved in a brief space of time, nor can it be imposed from outside. On the contrary, the attempt to achieve a more dynamic and innovative school organisation entails a willingness to work in the medium and long term, to confront existing problems, to take notice of all initiatives, to maintain a permanent atmosphere of evaluation and to consider the whole school approach as relevant.

Educational authorities' commitment to inclusive schools

To go ahead with inclusive schools is not simply the responsibility of teachers or of schools. It is a paramount decision of the educational authorities, which must send a clear message that inclusive schools could be, and must be, as good as the best schools.

This commitment to a school which is open to all runs parallel to that of rejecting other options which are detrimental for this kind of education: privatising schools; selecting children according to their abilities or for economical reasons; and only evaluating schools by their academic achievements.

But to be confident in good quality schools, open to all, calls for active work to improve the factors which encourage parents to choose inclusive schools. This intervention must aim at the following:

1. To allow more autonomy to these schools to adapt the curriculum and organise the pupils.

2. To supply more resources to these schools to give a better educational answer to all students, those with greater possibilities and those with lesser.

3. To establish a general priority for teachers in these schools, organising teacher training or ensuring that more professional opportunities exist in comparison with other schools.

4. To encourage these schools to design a more attractive educational project with more economic resources. For example, organising extra-curricular sport or more intensive foreign languages or specific classes for artistic development.

5. To send a clear message that these schools are looked after by the education authorities and are really quality schools.

6. To design a balanced evaluation model, which incorporates as determinant variables the socio-economic environment in which the school is situated and the resources the school has received. This model must include educational processes and results for pupils, parents, teachers and the community.

These are important tasks for educational authorities. They must work in those directions and when faced with different alternatives make those decisions which are in favour of inclusive schools. As it was affirmed in Salamanca, Spain, in the 1994 World Conference on Special Needs Education:

"The development of inclusive schools as the most effective means for achieving education for all must be recognised as a key government policy and accorded a privileged place on the nation's development agenda (...). While communities must play a key role in developing inclusive schools, government encouragement and support is also essential in devising effective and affordable solutions."

CHAPTER 4

INTEGRATION IN THE NETHERLANDS

by

Cor J.W. Meijer

Introduction

In the Netherlands special and regular education are fully separated so that care for children with all kinds of handicaps or special needs is located in special schools. These schools are directly funded according to the number of pupils they have. Thus the more children enrolled, the more money the schools receive. This is, among others, one of the main contributing factors why our special education structure is one of the largest in the world: about 5 per cent of all 4-12 year olds are educated in these schools.

Teachers, special needs professionals, policymakers and so on, are more or less looking forward expectantly to drastic changes in special education in the near future. How this will develop, in form and content, is outlined in the following sections.

The problem

Dutch policymaking in regular and special education over the last 10 to 15 years has been mainly distinguished by two types of special education schools which draw the highest numbers of children. These are schools for children with learning disabilities (with normal intelligence) and those for pupils with learning difficulties (with limited intelligence). These schools cater for about 70 per cent of the population of pupils with special needs (Central Bureau voor de Statistiek, 1993), and have grown substantially over the last decade. This trend has contributed to the current situation whereby 5 per cent of primary school children attend separate special schools.

Special education consists of schools for the different categories of handicaps. Table 1 illustrates the various types of school over a period of 10 years in percentages of the total pupil population, and clearly shows the Dutch situation. Not only the huge number of different types of school (15) but also the total percentage of children in segregated settings is distinct from the situation in many other countries (Pijl and Meijer, 1991). It is also clear that mild special needs contribute most to the situation, as can be seen from the percentages of learning disabled children and the one with learning difficulties, which together make up more than 3.5 per cent of the total population.

Table 1. **Percentages of children in special education**

	1981	1985	1989
Infants with developmental difficulties	0.05%	0.10%	0.17%
Deaf	0.07%	0.04%	0.03%
Hearing impaired	0.08%	0.09%	0.09%
Speech disorders	0.08%	0.12%	0.15%
Blind	0.01%	0.01%	0.01%
Partially sighted children	0.02%	0.01%	0.01%
Physically handicapped	0.15%	0.11%	0.10%
Children educated in hospitals	0.00%	0.05%	0.04%
Chronically ill	0.15%	0.12%	0.18%
Learning difficulties	**1.30%**	**1.35%**	**1.42%**
Severely mentally retarded	0.33%	0.37%	0.36%
Severely maladjusted	0.15%	0.16%	0.17%
Learning disabled	**1.47%**	**1.89%**	**2.11%**
Paedological institutes	0.04%	0.06%	0.07%
Multiple handicapped	0.05%	0.16%	0.19%
Total	**3.89%**	**4.54%**	**4.94%**

Source: Ministerie van Onderwijs en Wetenschappen, 1990.

The increase in special education referrals is clearly visible. When the aim of government policy to integrate special and ordinary education is measured according to the number of children being taught in an integrated setting, we must conclude that the Netherlands is not particularly successful in this field (Meijer, Pijl and Hegarty, 1994).

Since the late seventies, various educational projects have been set up in order to deal with a wider range of educational needs in regular education: teachers were trained and several experimental projects were implemented. However, as the table shows, this did not result in fewer referrals. Recently, a new analysis of the situation contributed to a different policy.

Analysis of the situation

A new government policy launched under the name "Together to school again" was introduced in 1990 (Ministerie van Onderwijs en Wetenschappen, 1990), based on an analysis of the educational factors as well as the system characteristics and policy aspects that are responsible for the current situation (Doornbos and Stevens, 1987, 1988). In line with the analysis of Madeleine Will in 1986 on integration efforts in the United States, the Dutch white paper distinguished the following:

1. Educational factors. Children differ from each other and it seems that these differences increase. Dutch schools cannot cope with these increasing differences. In spite of all the educational innovations in the last decades, it is clear that education is mainly directed at the average pupil. If there are too many children with special needs in a classroom, teaching becomes complicated. There is no support within the regular school itself. Support that is available is located outside the regular school building in special schools or by school counselling services and other support organisations. The only solution teachers see is to refer pupils with special needs to special schools where more professionals and time are available. However, there are continuously new groups of children requiring special help so it is a never-ending process. When teachers refer pupils to special education they are also largely left with a more homogeneous class of pupils to teach, and admit that this is one of the benefits of referral. In other words, they wish to keep their pupils' learning progress as far as possible at the same level, in homogeneous groups.

2. System factors. Special and regular education work independently so that it is the system itself that stimulates referrals. Special help is only available when children attend special schools. Even if part-time support could be a solution, the two-tier system lacks the flexibility to organise this, which means the child with special needs is taken to the special facility instead of the facility to the child. Responsibility for the pupil is transferred to another part of the educational system. Special education is an attractive option in this situation: there are special services for children with special needs. The present system makes it impossible for regular schools to help children. In this sense the services amplify the needs.

3. Policy factors. The funding system in the Netherlands prevents integration. The current situation is that the schools are financed separately. There is no incentive for regular education to cope with children who have special needs. The system also makes it attractive for special education to assess a referred child as eligible for special education, as the amount of time teachers and other professionals, psychologists for example, spend in special education is directly influenced by the number of children in a school. It is worth considering this so-called "paradox of legislation", which while proclaiming integration, in practice "rewards" the placement of children into separate special schools. In other words, we stimulate what we don't want. Funding is not linked to pupils but depends on the type of education they receive. Maintaining special needs children in regular schools is not encouraged. With the current system of integration is "punished".

A significant question to ask is, how do special schools differ from regular ones? Researchers have found many similarities in pupil characteristics, teaching methods, teacher behaviour, organisation and so on. It is difficult to trace obvious differences between the school types. This is also confirmed by the teachers themselves: certain special schools are similar to ordinary schools and the other way around. Education provision and its effectiveness are more or less the same in special and primary schools.

The solution

The Dutch government is now concentrating on alleviating this situation through a policy in which ordinary schools and schools for the learning disabled and those with learning difficulties co-operate on a regional level (Ministerie van Onderwijs en Wetenschappen, 1990, 1991). A first step towards this was to establish regional clusters of both ordinary and special schools. The clusters consist of one or more special schools working with a larger group of primary schools. This has resulted in every special and every ordinary school being attached to a nation-wide network of clusters. Most comprise about 20 to 40 schools, including two special schools. There are about 5 000 pupils in an average cluster, but it varies a lot: from over 10 000 per cluster to less than 500 in the smaller ones.

The second government tool to encourage integration is a new funding structure. The idea of this new system, is that a large part of the additional costs for special education will be allocated to the school clusters (instead of to the special school). School clusters may then decide to maintain the special provision in special schools. They could also decide to transfer parts of that provision to ordinary schools in some form or another. The key point is that ordinary schools participate in the decision-making process concerning the structure of special provision.

There are a few possible financial models here (Meijer, Peschar and Scheerens, 1995). The first ties resources to pupils (for example through a voucher system or client-centred budget). No matter where a pupil is educated, the resources follow the pupil. This appears to have certain disadvantages, however. It can result in time-wasting, bureaucratic registration procedures and the unnecessary labelling of children. Moreover, it can also work in the favour of the number of pupils considered to need special provision. The second model is based on allocating resources on the basis of the number of pupils within a certain school cluster, area or region, regardless of the number of children who have special education needs (the "budget system" or the "block-funding system" as it is known in New Brunswick, Canada). This system implies that there are no large regional differences regarding the frequency of special needs. In fact this model is also based on the conviction that differences in the number of pupils with special needs are largely determined by the extent of provision. In the Netherlands the funds will be allocated to a cluster of schools that decide together how the funds are to be used. More funding allocated to special schools results in less funding for integrated provision.

The question is whether this policy will foster the objective of integrating special and ordinary education. It must be said that without the necessary facilities (in terms of extra specialist help/time/attention) an inclusive policy has little chance of succeeding. In this sense, introducing a new funding structure is one of the necessary pre-conditions for integration. And when a new funding system is introduced, the setting up of school clusters is also a necessary pre-condition, as the size of the individual primary school is too small to arrange effective provision for children with special needs.

CHAPTER 5

FACTORS THAT INCLUSION MUST NOT OVERLOOK

by

Yerker Andersson

The learning process of human beings begins at birth and ends at death and occurs both inside and outside the classroom. This scientific conclusion has apparently not been universally accepted yet as school teachers still assume that education occurs mostly within the classroom. Social scientists (*e.g.* Bryjak and Soroka, 1994, pp. 102-131) have repeatedly found that the family, peer groups and pressure groups are important social factors, in addition to mass media, affecting the learning process. Yet, the advocates of educational innovations have too often tried to concentrate only on classroom activities in the learning process. The reason for this negligence probably is that it is easier to find strategies to manipulate classroom activities than social factors. Here I want to discuss the social factors that I believe inclusion should not overlook.

Parental involvement is a crucial factor for providing initial learning opportunities for children. Past elementary and secondary school experiences have, as the sociology of education suggests, been used as a starting point for parents to determine what resources can be used to provide learning opportunities for their children. They may be ready to determine the appropriateness of toys, books, and other learning materials for their children depending on the commonly given age categories they belong to. This parental knowledge may, however, be more severely limited if the parents discover that the educational needs of their children are different from theirs. Those parents with disabilities or having relatives with disabilities presumably have better access to information about disabilities, training opportunities, and organisations of persons with disabilities to provide appropriate early learning opportunities for children with a similar disability.

Several studies (Andersson, 1978; Meadow, 1968; Moores, 1971; Quigley and Frisina, 1961; Stevenson, 1964; Stuckless and Birch, 1966; and Vernon and Koh, 1972) have arrived at the same conclusion that deaf children of deaf parents tend to be more advanced in writing, reading, and speaking skills, compared to those of parents with normal hearing. From the sociological viewpoint, this finding should not be surprising precisely because deaf parents have been able to use their past school experiences for child-rearing in the same way as families with normal hearing do. In my opinion, schools in many countries have too often failed to adopt the past school experiences of parents with disabilities as a possible resource for parents of children with disabilities. My observation of a weekly discussion meeting between deaf and hearing parents in Sweden has convinced me that the past school experiences of deaf parents has enabled hearing parents to provide the most appropriate learning opportunities for their children. This self-helping process probably is more effective than the interventions by school professionals such as social workers, psychologists, or family therapists, possibly because the expertise of such professionals is less relevant than school experiences to the parents.

If children find that the school experiences of their parents are not relevant for their learning, they will likely seek other adults with more relevant school experiences. Such adults may be found through appropriate organisations, special schools, and informal groups. In sociology (*i.e.* Sullivan, 1995, pp. 94-95) such alternatives are called reference groups and peer groups which will be discussed below.

Sociology agrees that reference groups are another powerful agent in the learning process of children and adults. Special schools and religious, professional, ethnic, and other interest organisations have been used as examples of reference groups. The existence of such communities in virtually all societies gives a clear testimony about the importance of sharing experiences within a given group. This sharing pattern does not necessarily lead to segregation as long as human groups do not raise any physical or social barrier for each other.

On the basis of my international observations, I have a clear impression that educators in both industrialised and developing countries have no or inadequate knowledge about appropriate educational programs, organisations of persons with disabilities, independent living centres and other community centres. The boards of schools have even failed to consider persons with disabilities for possible membership. I believe that in co-operation with organisations of persons with disabilities, independent living centres, special schools and other community centres, parents and educators can acquire a better understanding of a particular disability and a working knowledge of the social life among persons with disabilities. For example, the appreciation of sign language or Braille as an educational tool certainly promotes parental or class interaction among deaf or blind children. Parental knowledge of technical devices such as text telephone, canes, wheelchairs is another important facilitating factor.

Local, state, and national organisations of people with disabilities in almost all industrialised and many developing countries again are excellent places where children with disabilities can learn how to acquire and improve their special skills. At an international congress for persons with disabilities, I have observed how individuals with different disabilities traded their own special strategies to overcome physical or social barriers. Like other skills such as the mastery of a spoken language, cooking, driving a car, the mastery of sign language or the skill to use technical devices can be improved only if individuals with similar disabilities have a chance to share and compare their newly acquired experiences.

The sharing pattern, described above, does not necessarily suggest that children with disabilities should abandon their parents in favour of adults, including those with disabilities, to whom they can relate themselves. In my opinion, the expansion of learning opportunities is more crucial than the selection of an appropriate learning opportunity simply because it will permit children to explore their own capacities more freely.

In virtually all societies, individuals seek moral support from other older or more experienced individuals to promote their own personal growth. In sociology (*viz.* Bryjak and Soroka, 1994, pp. 114-115), those providing such support are called peer groups. The formation of such groups is based on the mutual interests and capacities of individuals. Case histories have repeatedly shown the importance of peer groups for those individuals who wanted to promote their emotional, professional or social maturity. It is natural that individuals seek any individual with whom they can compare themselves. This comparison helps the individuals to become aware of what level their capacities can function best at. When they discover that their capacities are above average, compared to their peer groups, they will likely try to explore other groups whose capacities are more advanced. Such a natural search for peer groups has been found in virtually all countries. Neither educators nor parents can, of course, select or prescribe peer groups for children to join. Sociology, psychology and anthropology agree that it is not possible for any individual to grow outside groups. Hence, the adoption of peer groups is another factor that inclusion should not overlook.

The major problem I see in inclusion and other educational innovations, however, is the frequent failure of schools and other advocates to provide opportunities for children to relate their experiences to the appropriate school experiences of adults and to offer organisations of people with disabilities as possible reference groups and adults with disabilities as possible peer groups. This does not necessarily imply that disability should be used as a criterion in the placement of children in schools. I would instead argue that more consideration should be given to what learning opportunities the chosen school will likely be able to give children than to how well integrated each of the children will be. In fact, the degree of integration depends on the number of physical and social barriers within a given society and the societal tolerance of physical, mental and social variations.

CHAPTER 6

HOW SYSTEMIC ARE OUR SYSTEMIC REFORMS?[1]

by

Dianne L. Ferguson

Introduction

A remarkable amount has changed in education over the last twenty years. My own perspective on these changes emerges both from my experiences as an educator and as a parent. My son Ian, only gained access to public education after the passage of the Education of the Handicapped Act (P.L.-94-142) because our local public educators believed that the type, degree and multiplicity of his disabilities meant he was unable to learn enough to warrant participation in schooling. Access to public schools, however, did not then necessarily mean access to a public education. Our son, like thousands of other children and youth with significant disabilities, experienced separate classrooms, separate curricula, separate materials, and different teachers than all other participants in public schooling.

Although mainstreaming had been a substantial effort to change the delivery of special education services since the late 1960s, it was clear to my husband and me in the late 1970s that the possibility of mainstreaming was not available to our son. Indeed, the debates never considered students with severe disabilities. What the reform legislation had not changed were the underlying assumptions about schooling for students designated "disabled" that had engendered both, the mainstreaming debates, and the need for the Education of the Handicapped Act (EHA), in the first place.

Since special education emerged as a separate part of public education in the decades spanning the turn of the century, the fundamental assumptions about students and learning shared by both "general" and "special" educators has not really changed. These assumptions have become so embedded in the culture and processes of schools that they operate more as "truths" than assumptions. School personnel, families of school children, and even students themselves unquestioningly believe that:

- Students are responsible for their own learning.

- When students don't learn, there is something wrong with them.

---

1. An expanded version of this presentation has been published in Ferguson, D.L (1995), "The Real Challenge of Inclusion: Confessions of a Rabid Inclusionist", *Phi Delta Kappan*, Vol. 77 (4), pp. 281-287.

- Schools must determine what's wrong with as much precision as possible so that students can be directed to the track, curriculum, teachers and classrooms that match their learning ability profile. Otherwise no learning will occur.

Even efforts to "integrate", and later "include" students with severe disabilities in general education failed to challenge these fundamental assumptions. Indeed, these special education reforms have often failed to change very much at all.

Inclusion as "pretty good integration" at best

The current inclusion initiative has certainly resulted in some exciting and productive experiences for students. It has also produced other situations that are problematic and unsatisfying for everyone. As our son finished his official schooling and we all began his challenging journey to adult life, he enjoyed a couple of quite successful experiences, one as a real member of a high school drama class, despite still being officially assigned to a self-contained classroom (Ferguson, Meyer *et al.*, 1993). Ian's experiences in drama helped me begin to understand more fully than had his earlier experiences of part time integration, both that learning membership was the most important dimension of inclusion and that it was an extraordinarily complex phenomenon, especially within classrooms (Ferguson, 1994*a*). These experiences also prompted me to question other conventional wisdom about inclusion: Was it mostly about place? Must it be all the time? Was it okay for learning to take second priority to socialisation and friendship? Did one always have to be traded for the other? How would learning occur? Would students learn things that they could use and that would make a difference in their lives? Who would teach? What would happen to special educators? And more.

A three-year research effort later, I'd learned a good deal about what I thought inclusion was, and wasn't. Perhaps the most troubling realisation was that even when students were assigned to general education classrooms and spent most (or even all) of their time there with various kinds of special education supports, their presence and participation still often fell short of the kind of social and learning membership my son had achieved in one drama class, and that most inclusion proponents envisioned. Even to casual observers, some students seemed set apart -- immediately recognisable as different -- not so much because of any particular impairment or disability but because of what they were doing, with whom and how.

During the years of our research, my colleagues and I saw students walking through hallways with clip-board bearing adults "attached," or sitting apart in classrooms with an adult hovering over them showing them how to use different books and papers than anyone else in the class, even moving their hands to try to match what other students seemed to be doing by themselves. Often these "velcroed" adults were easily identifiable as "special" teachers because the students called them by their first names while using the more formal "Ms" or "Mr" to refer to the general education teacher. Students seemed in, but not of the class, so much so that we noticed teachers referring to particular students as "my inclusion student." It seemed to us that these students were caught inside a bubble that teachers didn't seem to notice, but that succeeded in keeping other students, and teachers, at a distance nevertheless.

We also saw students "fitting in," following the routines and looking more or less like other students in the class. But sometimes their participation seemed hollow. They looked like they were doing social studies, or math, but it looked more like "going through the motions" than a real learning engagement. Maybe they were "learning" in the sense of remembering things, but did they know what they were learning, we wondered? Or why? Or if they would use this learning in their lives outside this lesson?

Even the protection of the Individual Education Plan (IEP), a key component of EHA and now the updated IDEA (the Individuals with Disabilities Education Act), seemed yet one more barrier to real membership. Special education teachers became "teachers without classrooms", plying their teaching skills in lots of classrooms; deploying person-supports in the form of classroom assistants to teach; manage, and assist the "inclusion students" to meet IEP goals and objectives regardless of what might be happening with the rest of the class. Classroom teachers struggled to understand how to "bond" with their new students and the adults they brought with them. Even more challenging was how to negotiate teaching. The peripatetic special educator usually remained primarily responsible for writing IEPs that only distantly related to the classroom teacher's curriculum and teaching plans while at the same time pushing her to assume "ownership" of the student, often by following the instructions of the special educator, whether they were compatible with the general educator's teaching approach or not. Special educators who were successful at moving out of their separate classrooms struggled with the sheer logistics of teaching their students in so many different places. They also struggled with whether they were teachers of students or teachers of teachers and what might happen to them if the general educators ever "learned" how to include their students without their help.

Bursting bubbles

Gradually I came to see these examples and experiences that have been detailed elsewhere (Ferguson, Willis *et al.*, 1993; Ferguson and Meyer, in press) as problematic for everyone precisely because they failed to challenge underlying assumptions about student learning differences. Too much inclusion as implemented by special education seems to succeed primarily in relocating "special" education to the general education classroom along with all the "special" materials, specifically "trained" adults, and special curriculum and teaching techniques. The overriding assumptions remain clear and clearly communicated:

- These "inclusion" students are "irregular" even though they are in "regular" classrooms.

- They need "special" stuff that the "regular" teacher is neither competent nor approved to provide.

- The "special" educator is the officially-designated provider of these "special" things.

My colleagues and I also saw lots of positive examples like my son's experience in drama class. The challenge was to try to understand why. Gradually, I began to realise that if inclusion was ever to mean more than pretty good integration at best, we special educators would have to change our tactics. Resolving the various debates requires us to begin with the majority perspective and build the tools and strategies for achieving inclusion from "the center out" rather than from the most exceptional student in. Devising and defining inclusion to be about students with severe disabilities, indeed, any disabilities, seems increasingly wrong-headed to me and quite possibly doomed. It can only continue to focus everyone's attention on a small number of students, and a small number of student differences, rather than on the whole group of students with all their various abilities and needs.

The *real* challenge of inclusion

Realising the limits of inclusion as articulated by special educators was only part of my journey. It also took spending time in general education classrooms, listening to teachers, and trying to understand their struggles and efforts to change, to help me see the limits of general education as well. The general education environment, organised as it still is according to the Bell curve logic of ability labelling and grouping, may not be enough of an inclusive environment to ever achieve inclusion. It seems to me that the lesson to be learned from special education's inclusion initiative is that the real challenge is a lot harder, and more complicated, than we thought. Neither special nor general education has either the capacity or the vision alone to challenge and change the very deep rooted assumptions that separate and track children and youth according to presumptions about ability, achievement, and eventual social contribution. Meaningful change will require nothing less than a joint effort to reinvent schools that are more incorporative of all dimensions of human diversity. Change will also require that the purposes and processes of these reinvented schools be organised not so much to make sure that students learn and develop on the basis of their own abilities and talents, but rather to make sure that each child, regardless of their abilities or talents, is prepared to access and participate in the benefits of their communities so that others in that community care enough about what happens to them to value them as members (Ferguson, 1995; Asuto *et al.,* 1994).

My own journey to challenging these assumptions was greatly assisted by the elementary school faculty in one of our research sites. Most of our research up to that point had really centred on the perspectives of special educators. While we talked with lots of other teachers and staff, our access had always been through the special educator who was trying to move out into the school. Finally, however, we began to shift our attention to the whole school through the eyes of all its members. For me it was a shift from special education research to educational research that also happened to "include" consideration of special education teachers and students. I began to learn the language of schooling, became able to "talk education" rather than just special education and sought that same bilingualism for my students and colleagues through a series of newly re-framed research and demonstration projects.

Learning about various reform agendas within education, that support and facilitate a more systemic inclusion enormously reassured and encouraged me, and I have begun to refocus my efforts toward nurturing them. For example, in response to the changing demands of work and community life in the 21st century, reform and restructuring initiatives are focusing on students' understanding and use of their own learning rather than whether or not they can recall information during scheduled testing events. Employers and community leaders want citizens that are active learners and collaborators as well as individuals that possess the personal confidence and ability to contribute to a changing society (*e.g.*, Carnevale, Gainer and Meltzer, 1990).

As a consequence, teachers at all levels of schooling are trying to re-think the curriculum. From trying to cover a large number of subjects and "facts" to exploring a smaller number of topics of interest and relevance to students in more depth, teachers are looking for ways to help students not only acquire some essential information and capacities, but more importantly, to help them develop habits of learning that will serve them long after formal schooling ends (*e.g.*, Conley, 1993; Fogarty, 1991; Brooks and Brooks, 1993; Noddings, 1993; Sizer, 1992; Wiggens, 1989). An important aspect of this curriculum shift is that not all students will learn exactly the same things even within the same lesson or activity.

These changes in general education are being pursued because of increasing social complexity and student diversity. Educators are less and less confident that learning one standard, "official" curriculum will help students achieve the kind of competence they need to lead satisfactory lives. More and more educators are concerned not so much that some bit of knowledge content was learned, but rather that students use their learning in ways that make a difference in their lives outside school. One difficulty in making this happen day to day in classrooms is that students bring all manner of differences to the learning event that teachers must take into consideration. These include different abilities, of course, but also different interests, different family lifestyles and preferences about schools and learning. Students' linguistic backgrounds, socio-economic status and cultural heritage must also be considered as part of curriculum and teaching decisions. Finally, some students have different ways of thinking and knowing -- sometimes emphasising language, sometimes motor learning, or artistic intelligence, to name just three -- that can aid learning if teachers design experiences that draw out and use these various "intelligences" (Armstrong, 1994; Gardner, 1993; Leinhardt, 1992; Noddings, 1993).

To general education teachers, experimenting with these kinds of curriculum and teaching reforms, students with official disabilities become a difference in degree rather than type. Tailoring the learning event for them might require different adjustments, or more supports than for some other students. The essential process remains the same for all, achieving more, and more varied, learning outcomes for all students. Fears of "watering down" the official curriculum only remain for those classrooms that have not responded to the need for more systemic curriculum and teaching reform. Classrooms and teachers seriously engaged in preparing students for the future have already expanded and enriched the curriculum to respond both to the demands for broader student outcomes and to the different interests, purposes and abilities of each student.

A new inclusion initiative

These are just a few of the ongoing discussions within general education. There are many more. Some, like the pressure to articulate new state and national standards and benchmarks, are less clearly supportive of student diversity. Reform initiatives are emerging from all parts of the system -- from the efforts of small groups of teachers to state and federal policy makers. Often these various pressures for change contradict each other, but in the end all will have to be accommodated, understood and transformed into a single whole. Changing schools at all, never mind actually improving them, is an extraordinarily complex task.

Yet we run a great risk that all of this energy in general education, like our successive efforts in special education, will ultimately change very little. We need to avoid Cuban's (1984) assessment that "successive waves of educational reform are like storms that create violent waves on the surface but cause barely a ripple in the depths". My own efforts to achieve a more systemic change have led me to advocate for my own definition of inclusion:

Inclusion is a process of meshing general and special education reform initiatives and strategies in order to achieve a unified system of public education that incorporates all children and youth as active, fully participating members of the school community, that views diversity as the and that achieves a high quality education for each student by assuring meaningful effective teaching, and necessary supports for each student.

As I and others who share this broader understanding work to create genuinely inclusive schools, we will be encouraging people throughout schools to change in three directions. The first involves the shift away from organising and structuring schools according to ability toward a structure that begins with student diversity and creates many different ways of organising students for learning. This shift will also require teachers with different abilities and talents to work together to create a wide array of learning opportunities (Darling-Hammond, 1993; Oakes and Lipton, 1992; Noddings, 1993; Skrtic, 1991).

The second shift involves moving away from teaching approaches that emphasise the teacher as disseminator of content and require students only to retain that content, to approaches that emphasise the role of the learner as well as the teacher in creating knowledge, competence, and ability that is useful, used, and leads children and youth to seek the answers to more questions. There is a good deal of literature that seeks to blend together various theories of teaching and learning into a flexible and creative approach to the design of teaching and the pursuit of learning in this way. The strength of these approaches is that they begin with an appreciation of student difference that can be stretched comfortably to incorporate the differences of disability as well as much of the effective teaching technology created by special educators (Conley, 1993; Fogarty, 1991; Brooks and Brooks, 1993; Noddings, 1993; Sizer, 1992; Wiggens, 1989).

The third shift involves re-conceptualising what schools do for individual students from providing an educational service, to providing educational supports for learning. This shift occurs naturally as a consequence of the changes in teaching demanded by diversity. Valuing diversity and difference, rather than trying to change or diminish it so that everyone fits into some ideal of similarity, leads to the realisation that we can support children and youth to be active members of their communities now. The opportunity to participate in life no longer must wait until some standard of "normalcy" or similarity is reached through our efforts to "fix" or "minimise" deficits. Support also encourages a shift from viewing difference or disability in terms of individual limitations to a focus on environmental constraints. Perhaps the most important feature of support as a concept for schooling is that it is grounded in the perspective of the person receiving it, not the person providing it (Ferguson, Hibbard *et al.,* 1990; Smull and Bellamy, 1991).

Are our reforms systemic enough? I think not yet. Our real challenge is to create schools in which our day to day efforts no longer assume that a particular text, activity, or teaching mode will "work" to support any particular student's Learning. Instead we must construct and adopt the new assumptions that will create a new reality of reinvented inclusive schools where a constant conversation between students and teachers, school personnel, families, and community members, to construct learning, document accomplishments and adjust supports.

CHAPTER 7

WHAT WE KNOW ABOUT SCHOOL INCLUSION

by

Gordon L. Porter

Introduction

What is inclusionary education? Inclusionary education is a system of education in which students with disabilities are educated in neighbourhood schools in age-appropriate regular classroom settings with non-disabled peers. They are provided with supports and instruction based on their individual strengths and needs. The inclusion of students with significant disabilities in regular classrooms in regular schools is a controversial area of educational practice in many jurisdictions at this time (Porter and Richler, 1990).

Inclusion has become controversial because it involves a fundamental change in the approach taken to the education of students with disabilities. For many people, it requires not only a change in approach and practice, but also a re-thinking of fundamental attitudes about education. The focus on student disability and deficiency which predominated in the past has been challenged to shift to a broader focus -- one that emphasises the need to examine the "defects" not of the student but of the school and the classroom (Skrtic, 1991). With this approach, the emphasis is on the ways in which educational practices can be improved and the school can fulfil the goal of providing a supportive and nurturing environment for all students.

It is hard to make change in a well developed system with high levels of belief in the need for specialisation and normalisation, in other words a *"sophisticated stage"*. In most jurisdictions in developed countries, the special education system is very sophisticated and thus immune to change like that demanded to achieve inclusion. In New Brunswick, the Special Education system was at a relatively less developed or *"primitive stage"*, and thus required less change. Change in Special Education practice is easier where there is reliance on generalists, that is, when it is at a more primitive level (Sage, 1989).

Inclusion requires a re-thinking of the traditional approach to Special Education Services. The traditional approach was based on a process that involved assessment of student disability, diagnosis of the specific aspects of the child's disability, followed by prescription, programming and placement. This process inevitably led to some special arrangement -- a special class, a pull-out resource program, or, in some cases, segregated schools or institutional placements. The following table illustrates the contrast between the traditional and inclusive approach to education.

Table 2. **Special education practice: two perspectives**

Traditional View	Inclusion View
Focus on student	Focus on classroom
Expert assessment	Collaborative problem-solving
Special program for the student defined	Strategies for the teacher
Placement in a special program	A responsive and effective classroom

Source: Porter (1995).

The traditional approach suffered from a number of weaknesses that have resulted in demands for reform. New Brunswick's schools have been in the forefront of this movement. The closure of the William F. Roberts Hospital School, a children's institution, in 1985, and the dismantling of the Auxiliary School System are examples of this reform (Porter, 1986).

The movement towards inclusion is based on a completely different perspective on how special education should operate. In an inclusionary approach, the regular class is assumed to be the appropriate instructional setting for all students. The school is committed to making the regular class work. Teachers are provided with the support and assistance required to permit them to meet each student's needs. Assistance is provided through peer collaboration as teachers work together to solve instructional problems. The child's particular needs are looked at on an individual basis and an appropriate program is established that provides needed supports to both the student and the teacher.

The inclusive approach views the classroom as an adaptive, supportive environment -- one which is responsive to every child's needs. It does not see the student with a disability as a patient in need of a cure. It sees the classroom, with a student with a disability included, as an environment that needs support.

Since the move toward inclusion has been such a change to the traditional way schools, teachers, parents, and others have thought about student's with disabilities, it is no surprise to note the considerable controversy around this issue. In this paper, the findings made during several years of working with such an approach in New Brunswick are described.

Peer perspectives on inclusion

The perspective of students offers an interesting way to view this question of inclusion. The results of two surveys of student perspective provide a view of the issue from the participants themselves and are thus useful in understanding this experience in a unique way.

The first survey was completed when inclusion was still a new phenomenon in New Brunswick schools (District 12, 1987). Late in the school year 49 students in a Junior High School were surveyed. The students were in grade 8 and were asked to reflect on the experience of being in regular classes with students with special needs for the first time. Both quantitative and qualitative results were obtained based on the four main questions asked. Quantitative results were as follows:

Questions	Yes	No	Not sure
1. Do you feel that students with special needs should be in the regular classroom?	92%	6%	2%
2. Were you able to work in class without interference by the student with special needs?	82%	10%	8%
3. Did you work with the student in class or at other times?	67%	33%	
4. Do you feel you have learned anything from having a student with special needs in your class?	76%	24%	

In reference to question two on interference in the classroom by student's with special needs, the students added the following qualitative comments:

"She is different and may disturb us a little, but it doesn't bother me."
"She interferes some but not as much as some other people do."

In reference to question one concerning whether students with special needs should be in the regular classroom, the following comments were added by those who responded positively:

"It is a learning experience."
"She is learning to fit in."
"We can learn from her."
"She has the same rights as I do."
"People are people whether they are handicapped or not."
"She is a person too."
"It is good for me to get used to a person with special needs."
"They need to be brought up in the same environment."

Comments added by those who responded negatively included the following:

"They don't learn what we do."
"Being around grade 8 students does her more harm than good."

In response to question 4, students indicated they had learned the following things by having students with special needs in their classroom:

"They have the same needs as us."
"I used to laugh at them."
"We have to be more careful about what we do so she won't pick up any bad habits."
"They aren't as bad as we thought."
"I learned to be kind."
"You have to care for people's feelings no matter who they are."
"We need to have respect for everyone."
"We should treat them the same as others but sometimes it is hard."
"If I ever have children with special needs or work with children with special needs, I now know how they feel and how I feel, and I can cope with it."

The comments of students noted above show a level of maturity, that at times, we erroneously believe adolescents do not possess. In assessing how inclusion affects students, it is important that their opinions be asked rather than thrusting the beliefs of an adult world on them -- an adult world, it should be remembered, that provided limited exposure to children or adults with disabilities.

The second survey was completed several years later at a high school (District 12, 1989). It involved 70 students from classrooms where students with special needs were inclusionary.

Questions	Yes	No	Not sure
1. Did inclusion take away from your learning time?	2%	91%	7%
2. Was there some learning for the inclusionary student?	94%	2%	4%
3. Was there disruptive behaviour that interfered with your learning?	3%	72%	25%
4. Do you feel there were adequate supports provided for this student?	97%	3%	0%
5. Do you feel the regular classroom is the place for every student?	66%	34%	0%

It is clear that the issue of interference with learning is not a concern to either junior or high school students. Students with disabilities were not a liability to others learning in these classrooms. As well, the results for question 5, on whether every student should be in the regular classroom, warrant analysis. While the clear majority in both groups were in favour of all students being there (Junior High: 92 per cent and High School: 66 per cent), the lower results among high school students are intriguing.

One possibility is that the students in high school have less intensive contact with students with disabilities since they have a different mix of peers in each class. It is also possible that students consider out-of-class placement such as those in work placements in the community as desirable.

Finally, the high school results illustrate something observed frequently in the implementation of an inclusive school program -- individuals demonstrate a very positive attitude toward inclusion of students with disabilities who they know first-hand. Note the overwhelmingly positive answers to the questions that rely on direct experience. It is when people are asked to extend their experience and generalise it, that more doubt creeps in. The results of these student surveys are encouraging. They hold promise for a more sensitive, accepting and equitable society in the future.

School practices

It is not surprising that teachers are apprehensive about teaching students with severe disabilities in their classes. Research conducted in New Brunswick schools indicates that teachers need to have direct experience with inclusion for their attitudes to change (Porter, 1991). Theoretical discussions and preparatory training sessions may be helpful but they seem to have little effect until the teacher actually has a student with disabilities in class. Teachers need to get to know the student and directly experience the benefits the student gets from inclusionary education. One New Brunswick educator said this on the subject :

> *Teachers definitely need experience with special needs students. One teacher who has a special needs student this year was (...) really nervous and very uptight about it (...) in September. Since it was his first year he depended on me almost 100% during September, and into October. But now he's enjoying this student. He comes to me probably, two or three times a week, to ask a question. But he's taken the student as one of his own and has come on a lot more than I had even hoped. Experience does make a difference. They have to have a year under their belts before some of the fear is going to be alleviated* (Porter, 1991, p. 138).

The acceptance of inclusion grows with experience, but it doesn't eliminate teacher's concerns about a number of very practical matters. One teacher interviewed pointed out that classroom teachers become more anxious and concerned about inclusion as class size gets larger. Teachers are also concerned about having students with severe behaviour problems in their classes. This includes students who are physically aggressive or self-abusive. They express concern about the effect students with distracting or disrupting behaviours have on other students and their ability to pay attention and benefit from instruction.

However, the direct experience mentioned earlier seems to be the key to eliminating a fear of the unknown. Here is a second description of this:

> *A lot of times they have to see the success before their attitude is going to change. I had Special Ed. Kids in my class right from my first day of teaching. As a result I was more accepting and couldn't understand why people weren't accepting inclusion. I think until they've been through it, until they have a student in their class and have the experience, then, they'll accept it wasn't that bad* (Porter, 1991, pp. 151-153).

Once the teacher gets to know the student and starts to experience the success of inclusion, attitudes start to change. Direct experience shows teachers that many of the things feared don't actually materialise.

This brings to point the contrast between the teacher's role in an inclusive school and a special education program based on segregated classes and programs. In an inclusive school, the classroom teacher is the "direct" service provider. Other staff members may assist and provide support, but the classroom teacher is the professional directly responsible for the child's learning and success. This is clearly illustrated in the following table.

DIRECT SERVICE	INDIRECT SERVICE & COLLABORATIVE SUPPORT
THE REGULAR CLASSROOM TEACHER	*The M&R* Teacher* *Teacher Assistant* *Guidance Counsellor* *School Administrator* *District Staff* * (Methods and resources)

Research in New Brunswick has identified an interesting ambiguity between the way some teachers talk about inclusion and the way they act. A support teacher's observation:

> *Even though you hear them saying things against it (inclusion), their actions don't support what they're saying. I think people are still afraid of saying in front of their peers? Well, maybe it's not such a bad thing.' They've been saying that it's so terrible now for two years that they can't lose face and say that maybe their attitude has changed* (Porter, 1991).

The attitudes of teachers in New Brunswick have been changing for the positive. One support teacher carried out a survey of the opinions of teachers in their school concerning inclusion. Twenty-four of the 30 teachers completed and returned the forms, and 22 of these 24 teachers said they felt students with disabilities should be included. Only two of the 24 indicated they did not agree. Of the 24, 12 said that their attitudes had changed and 9 of these 12 reported that their attitudes were more positive. Most of the comments were positive, although a few continued to have sceptical attitudes about the inclusion process.

Inclusion: a challenge to educators

Inclusive education requires a commitment to both excellence and equity by school officials and policy makers. It is a major challenge to both teachers and school administrators and requires new school and classroom practices (Fullan, 1991*b*). In addition, strategies to support classroom teachers in solving problems are a priority. In New Brunswick, the critical innovations that have supported inclusive practice are the strategies briefly described below.

The method and resource teacher model

In New Brunswick, a key element in the successful move to schools that can support inclusive programs is the new role that was developed for the "special educator". With direct practice in the hands of regular class teachers, the "special educator" can assume a collaborative consultation model to provide support to classroom colleagues.

The name given to this position is "The Method and Resource Teacher" (Porter, 1991). Each school is assigned one or more of these positions depending on the level of support needed. This teacher is school-based, and almost always does better with a background that includes successful regular teaching experience. An essential aspect of the work is an orientation to active and persistent problem-solving at the school level. An ability to work well with adults, teachers, principals and parents, is also important. A job description of the Method and Resource (M&R) Teacher is contained in the following table.

In day-to-day practice, M&R teachers spend a majority of their time collaborating with teachers. They assist in planning, preparing and monitoring programs. They observe in the classroom and assist the teacher with specific needs of individual students. The M&R teacher must schedule and monitor teacher-assistants and volunteer helpers. They also spend a great deal of time consulting with parents, guidance counsellors, administrators and others.

Job Description: Method and Resource Teacher

M&R teachers consult and collaborate with teachers, parents and other personnel and/or agencies to assure student success in learning.

Responsibilities:

- Collaboration with school and district staff, parents and outside agencies;
- Liaison with school and district staff, parents and outside agencies;
- Program development;
- Monitoring;
- Personal growth and professional development

Source: Porter (1991).

Other activities of the M&R teacher include completing academic assessments and other diagnostic procedures with individual students. They also need to provide leadership in dealing with crisis situations that arise with specific students. Classroom teachers simply do not have time to do all of the paper work associated with students with disabilities. Inevitability, the M&R teacher must complete the paperwork related for Individual Educational Plans (IEPs) and other associated matters. Finally, most M&R teachers spend time doing things every teacher must do, like hallway supervision, bus duty and providing staff support for other student and school activities.

Staff development and training strategies

The implementation of inclusive classroom programs requires a major effort to provide instructional and support staff with training and planning opportunities. The efforts include learning new instructional strategies as well as new processes and procedures to design and plan lessons and to find solutions to problems.

The prime teaching approach used to support inclusive education in New Brunswick is multi-level *instruction* (Collicott, 1991). The "multi-level instruction model" assumes the inclusion of all students in regular classes. Since classrooms now contain students with varying levels of skill and ability, teachers are challenged with the task of restructuring their classroom practice. The focus is not on special or separate activities for students with special needs but on inclusion and participation with their peers. In inclusive classrooms, the mandate to teachers is to include *all* students in the context of the instruction taking place in the regular classroom. The teacher plans for all students within one lesson and thus is able to weave individual goals into the classroom curriculum. Through the use of a variety of instructional strategies the necessity for separate programs is decreased.

As an alternative to preparing and teaching a number of different lessons within a single class, teachers must develop a framework for planning that allows for one main lesson with varying methods of presentation, practice and evaluation.

To develop a unit or a lesson that is truly multi-level the teacher must have a firm grasp of the aim of the lesson. It must include a variety of teaching techniques aimed at reaching all levels of students. This means considering student learning styles when planning presentation methods, involving students in the lesson through questioning aimed at different levels of thinking (i.e., Bloom's Taxonomy), allowing some students to have adjusted expectations, providing for student choice in the method of demonstrating understanding of the concept being taught, accepting that these different methods are of equal value, and evaluating students based on their individual differences.

Staff development

One of the most consistent practices introduced during the implementation of inclusion was the commitment to *on-going training* for M&R teachers (Collicott and Porter, 1992). At first, bi-weekly sessions were held one afternoon per week, and although this has changed to one full day session per month, the investment in time for training and problem-solving among these teachers has been viewed as beneficial. Method and resource teachers have also been supported to take part in a wide-range of training at universities, conferences, seminars and other professional gatherings. Training for classroom teachers has also been given high priority. This training has been province wide as well as at the district and school level. The training has included a range of topics, such as classroom teaching strategies, information on specific disabilities, assessment and diagnostic approaches.

School teams

Over time, the implementation of an inclusive school program led to the development of what is now called a "School-based Student Services Team". During the early stages, it was not clear just how important this team would be to the success of the inclusion effort. At first, the M&R teacher was expected to be responsible for the success or failure of the program. The support of the principal, vice-principal, guidance counsellor and other teachers was considered beneficial but could not be taken for granted at this initial stage. Over time it became clear that schools which experienced the highest degree of success were those that had the highest degree of involvement and support from the school support team. This naturally lead to the identification of a school-based Student Services Team with responsibility for supporting teachers and students in a systematic way.

The team typically consists of the principal, vice-principal, M&R teacher(s), guidance counsellor(s), teacher assistant, and on occasion, other staff. The teams meet on a weekly basis for 60 to 90 minutes. They discuss issues regarding students, difficulties that teachers may be experiencing, and other relevant matters. The team members share impressions, set priorities, assign responsibilities, and establish tasks to be completed before the next meeting. A consistent and creative approach to problem-solving is the key to the success of the school team in the inclusive education model. The effective functioning of the team has been a clear indication of school's effectiveness in overall terms and not just in the area of special education.

The role of the principal

Much has been said about the challenge school inclusion creates for the classroom teacher. Experience in New Brunswick indicates that the school principal is at least as critical, to the success of inclusion, as the teacher (Porter, 1991, p. 129). This should not be surprising, since educational research has shown the great influence the principal has over the changes that occur in schools. The principal must consistently be involved in sharing the vision of inclusion with staff, parents and the general public, and must provide moral and instructional support for teachers during a time of changing classroom practice. The principal must link the success of inclusion to good instructional strategies and procure additional supports needed to guarantee the success of teachers and students. Principals must show leadership in resolving organisational or administrative problems. They need to participate in planning meetings, particularly those involving students with challenging needs. The principal needs to be fully aware of critical situations before they become serious problems. An example follows:

> *The principal has to really know what is going on. He has to (...) believe in the program. Because, if you have little breakdowns, you have to have the support in order to say "Look, it's going to work, we just need to work on it a little harder." You have to have the back-up all the way down the line, otherwise the system will fail* (Porter, 1991, p. 130).

The principal needs to listen to concerns and take action. Teachers need to know that the principal is positive about the program and is fully behind efforts to make it successful. A teacher describes a situation where the principal's role is clear:

> *A student was placed in a classroom where the teacher wasn't really sold on the idea. The principal said, "We've really got to make this situation work, because if it doesn't, it will make it difficult for all of us." So the principal and I have gone out of our way to make sure the program has been a successful experience for the teacher. We've involved her in workshops and had her take time out and it's worked very well. The teacher now believes that it (inclusion) is working and can see changes in the student* (Porter, 1991, p. 129).

Another gave this example:

> *A teacher was having a lot of misgivings about having an exceptional student in the room. I had a hard time convincing her that she had to play a part in meeting the needs of the student. She didn't feel she could do that, so I left it at that point. I didn't feel it was my role to push it with her any more. I talked to the principal and asked him to assess the situation from his point of view. In his regular classroom visitation, he was able to get the same point across and after a few weeks the teacher was coming to me and saying "I worked with him (the child) today and it was great"* (Porter, 1991, p. 129).

That principal turned what could have been a difficult situation into a positive one. This level of support is not always present. One teacher was clearly unhappy with the leadership and interest taken by the principal. Her comments:

> *If he was interested (in the program) it would help. But since the beginning of the year there has been nothing said. If the principal brought it up, teachers would see that he's monitoring it to see how it's going. He could even go into the classes where special needs students are (...). He could ask the teachers how they're doing with the program. It would be so much more effective if it was him, rather than me* (Porter, 1991, pp. 139-140).

This statement depicts the principal's capacity to have a negative as well as a positive influence on the effort to implement inclusionary programs for students with disabilities. Whether through lack of initiative, interest or confidence, the principal can seriously undermine the program.

Schools need motivated, enthusiastic, and effective principals and teachers with the confidence to do the job well. Our experience is that principals can provide the positive support and leadership teachers need to meet the challenge of integrating students with disabilities.

One of the teachers interviewed had previously been an Auxiliary Class teacher. She told us this:

There was a time when I distrusted regular education. I would never have allowed a child who had special needs to go into a regular school system because I thought it would kill them. But after seeing that it could work and being part of it and seeing the change in the children, naturally I had to change my attitude. I always believed in individualised education, but I wasn't sure the school system could do that. I didn't trust it to make those changes. But now I can see -- I mean it stares me in the face everyday -- that schools can change, that teacher practice can change (Porter, 1991, p. 141).

District student services team

In addition to the school based support team, a District Student Services Team has also been put in place. The district team provides support to the schools to assure the provision of a quality education in an inclusive setting for all students. Some of the responsibilities of the team are instructional, while others are purely collaborative and supportive. Members of the team monitor school programs, provide needed support to school staff, attend weekly school team meetings as a liaison person, and conduct training with M&R teachers, guidance counsellors, teachers and support staff.

The District Student Services support team consists of the Director of Student Services, one or more student services consultants, school psychologist, school social workers, speech-language pathologists, transition-to-work co-ordinator, an itinerant teacher for the visually impaired and an itinerant teacher for the hearing impaired. The team is characterised by its members' ability to collaborate with one another and with school personnel, the mutual respect they show for other professionals in the field and for their commitment to a problem solving approach. The district team must be deeply committed to achieving the goals of inclusive education and improving the quality of instruction for all students. The team by necessity must be flexible and creative in the strategies used with schools, teachers and students. A great deal of time must be spent on proactive planning to anticipate and be prepared for new issues and challenges.

Reinforcing attitudinal change

Many educators, including special educators, continue to feel sceptical and anxious about inclusive educational programs. They question the capacity of regular school programs to accept and provide for special needs students. However, a new and optimistic view is not uncommon. Nearly all M&R teachers, most of them experienced classroom teachers feel very positive about their work. They believe that inclusion is working and that the support role they play is an important element in making it work. They get satisfaction out of facilitating the success of others. The M&R teachers see inclusion enriching and enhancing the lives of students with disabilities. They provide enthusiastic affirmation that inclusion is good educational practice.

One teacher said it this way:

Seeing the changes! I've gotten a lot of satisfaction just seeing the improvements in students who, when they arrived in September, I thought? What are we going to do with this child?' And then seeing inclusion is working. Seeing the support of the staff and administration and students. We've had so many students who have taken it upon themselves to make it work. It's working well, I think. You can see the differences in the children (Porter, 1991, p. 141).

And another teacher:

Seeing the results! When you actually see a student progressing you feel good about it because chances are that progress would not have taken place unless there had been intervention of some kind and that's when you feel good. When you watch a student with special needs with friends around, going on her own to the cafeteria, not even requiring assistance, you feel good. When you watch a student who comes in and we were informed in advance that it's going to be very difficult, and that student can go for two or three or four weeks and actually be a part of the classroom situation and cope, you feel good. Last year I thought I'd just get the year over and then I'd go back to my home room class, but by March with all the help that everyone was giving and seeing the results that we were seeing, I thought?, No! I'm going to stick with it and try another year.' And I'm glad I did (...). Right now I feel that we are accomplishing something (Porter, 1991, pp. 137-138).

While most teachers have accepted that inclusion is probably in the child's best interest they are apprehensive about what they are expected to teach the student with special needs. Some teachers are concerned that classroom inclusion will result in the student missing out on the benefits of more individualised instruction they thought was received previously. One teacher with experience teaching a segregated class suggested that this was because teachers imagine that something could be done in that setting that can't be done in the regular class. As she said "they don't understand that what you do on a one-to-one situation is basically what would take place in the regular classroom."

Teachers said that while inclusion benefits students with disabilities it also can have a positive effect on general education. One of the teachers addressed this issue as follows:

I think the biggest thing that we've done, other than inclusion, is to make teachers aware of the fact that all children are not learning at grade level. They have to be teaching them at the level they're at and having them meet with success at that level. And I think that's happening a lot more that it ever happened before (...). A lot of children are having their needs met (who) before would have just been pushed along or ignored. But now they aren't ignoring them. Teachers are quite conscious of the fact that they're on a different program and they're addressing the whole situation differently (Porter, 1991).

While inclusion is proceeding with substantial evidence of success some teachers continue to be apprehensive. They continue to nurture the idea that the movement towards inclusion will go away. One teacher stated :

There are still people who are saying it's a cycle. It's going to come around again and we're going to do away with all this inclusion. I don't think it's a cycle. I don't think it's going to come around. I think that things are evolving (...). Next year we'll do things a little differently, but it's going to be improving on what we're doing now. We're never really going to segregate those children and go back to the system we had before. I think that new teachers and teachers who have been involved realise that. I think parents are too aware of the situation to let it go back (Porter, 1991).

New Brunswick has made considerable progress toward achieving an inclusionary school program for all students. This has been a major challenge that has not been easy. It has been difficult for parents, students and educators. The debate and discussion, predictable as it may be to those familiar to the research on the process of change, has been confusing and of concern to parents and the public. However, working with principals, teachers and students provides a basis for optimism about the on-going success of inclusion. Research into the positive change that can occur in teacher and student attitudes is encouraging (Perner and Porter, 1996). Inclusion requires teachers to make a firm commitment to every child and to their education. It assumes and demands the personal growth and development of students and teachers. Finally, it promotes a positive perspective about public education in general and about the learning potential of individual staff and students.

CHAPTER 8

THE CHANGING ROLES OF SCHOOL PERSONNEL IN A RESTRUCTURED AND INCLUSIVE SCHOOL

by

Kolbrún Gunnarsdóttir

This paper presents views on the subject of the changing roles of school personnel in a restructured and inclusive school and of some of the factors that have brought about these changes.

During the last four or five decades the school has changed from being a school for most children to being a school for all. The definition of a school for all is not the same in all countries, but in most OECD countries it is the same -- a school where there is a place for all -- an inclusive school.

The use of language tells us how the general public views different phenomena. This is especially noticeable when people with handicap are concerned. In my language, Icelandic, which is very transparent, the word integration is not used. Instead we use an Icelandic word which means mixing together. With new words and concepts in every field, a language problem can arise. In the educational field the word "*inclusion*" has now created a problem. A proper word has not been found so the concept "a school for all" has more meaning in my country than inclusion. In my vocabulary, an inclusive school, is a school for all.

The changes in the schools go hand in hand with the changes of views on disability and services offered to people with disabilities.

At the time when all children with disabilities were first accepted in the school system, in accordance with the 1974 law on compulsory education in Iceland, they were carefully diagnosed according to their disability and each group had their own special school. Within their schools the teachers became experts on different disabilities. In due course, views and ideas changed and teaching became more oriented towards the child rather than its disability. All this time research went on and the experts and the general public alike became more understanding of different disabilities. With increased understanding more people, people with handicap, parents, teachers and other experts asked themselves the question "why can children with disabilities not attend the same schools as ordinary children?"

Today it is widely accepted that children and young people with disabilities have the same right to attend the same schools as their peers without disabilities and receive education, each according to his or her ability. The 1995 law on compulsory education in Iceland makes no mention of special education but pupils that need assistance are entitled to it in their schools. Regulations are written to ensure this. In a school for all the question of special education as such has to be answered. Does special education exist in a school for all? If the school performs according to the main aims of the law on compulsory schools where every pupil shall be educated according to his/her interests and development, we do not need special education, but rather special pedagogy. This is an interesting problem. Is there a fundamental difference between special pedagogy and ordinary pedagogy?

It has been maintained that special pedagogy is an independent discipline with its roots in pedagogy, psychology, philosophy, sociology, medicine and linguistics (the Association of Icelandic Special Teachers, 1994). On the other hand it has been argued that special pedagogy can be called a practical version of pedagogy (Porsteinsson, 1995). Following that argument, special education teachers are teachers that have further education in pedagogy with a speciality in teaching children and young people with disabilities of different character. These teachers need both insight and practical knowledge for given situations.

With the new Icelandic law on compulsory education from 1995 the teacher's role has changed.

Today the teacher has to be able to work in at least three different levels of curriculum; the national curriculum, the school curriculum and class and individual curricula. But how has the teacher's role changed?

In the past, a special teacher had to be able to identify and evaluate different educational needs, and to have enough knowledge in the disciplines already mentioned to know which experts to turn to when further evaluations and opinions were needed. The special teacher had to know how to put all this information together and create a teaching situation, either within or outside of the ordinary classroom. A special teacher knew more than an "ordinary" teacher about teaching some pupils, *i.e.* was better at making individual curricula for children with learning difficulties or physical disabilities. The special teacher had to know what was different in the way children with those disabilities learn and why. But the basic skills were the same. The different approaches lay in the knowledge of how to work out a curriculum for the children.

In a school for all, the teacher has to be able to do all these things and take the whole class into account as well. So today more demands are made on a class teacher in a school for all than on an ordinary teacher in an ordinary school or a special teacher in a special school 20-25 years ago.

It is still the case that some pupils may have to leave their own home school for a period of time to attend a special school. The reasons are many. For example, a pupil may need teaching methods which require new technology that is only available at one place in a country or a cluster of countries, or environmental factors may make it impossible for the child to be in a particular school for a shorter or longer period of time. Education systems must also be aware of the need to develop expertise in teaching methods for pupils with special needs as well as other pupils.

Does special pedagogy exist when the school has become a school for all? If the argument that special pedagogy is an independent discipline holds, then special pedagogy will continue to exist. The situation becomes more complicated if it is maintained that special pedagogy as an independent discipline does not exist. There is, for example, the crisis that special teachers meet as a profession when the school has become a school for all. This is especially true if special pedagogy does not have a theory of its own, but builds its knowledge on intuition or is a mixture of theories.

CHAPTER 9

THE QUALITY OF INTEGRATION DEPENDS ON THE QUALITY OF EDUCATION FOR EVERYBODY

by

August Dens

Introduction

As an introduction I wish to affirm that the quality of integration depends directly on the quality of teaching and learning; actually I should say *learning and teaching*, in this order. Saying this I refer to an educational environment, taking care of the capacities and needs of all pupils, included those pupils who need specific approaches and interventions. The evaluation of quality has always been a fundamental concern in all sectors of society, including education. However, with changes in, and the development of, attitudes it is necessary to develop new parameters for evaluating the quality of education.

The *traditional approach* for evaluating quality is the degree with which the product conforms to certain goals and standards. Within that framework it was quite simple to evaluate quality, taking into account the prevailing features which were dominating the traditional structures in education. For example:

- the centralisation of the educational system;
- the precise legal framework in the organisation and the curriculum;
- the nature and composition of exams, whether regional or even national, organised to judged quality; and
- an influential inspectorate, with access to all schools, empowered to monitor the delivery of lessons to all pupils.

The new approach for evaluation of quality is more concerned with an analysis of educational *processes*. I refer to the process of learning and the different factors that facilitate the learning. This vision implies that teaching is like a succession of dynamic and interactive events, individually or groupwise, in which the pupil is the principal actor in his learning.

To judge the quality of integration using this new approach, three sets of factors need to be considered: social factors, personnel factors and factors relating to teaching.

Factors relating to the social situation

Above all it is necessary to change *attitudes* current in society, and particularly in education. Schools have to address the theme of how pupils with either a moderate or severe disability can participate fully in life, and in school. However it is normal that an unknown or a new situation causes feelings of insecurity. This is a strong factor in the resistance to change, which we can meet in some of our administrations or teacher unions. One way of changing attitudes is by promoting good practice, for example through the exchange and co-operation activities offered by this OECD study.

Legislation may change attitudes. Appropriate legislation respects the fundamental right of integration. This means:

- the right to education;
- the right to equal opportunities; and
- the right to participate in the life of society.

Effective *political approaches* are based on the appreciation of the interactive nature of disability. Politicians responsible for making laws need to set realistic objectives. It is clearly established that politicians cannot determine the success of their initiatives through the number of children remaining in special schools. It has to be more positive. The aim should be enhancing the quality of education for all pupils in mainstream schools, creating a viable alternative to special school education. Politicians should state clearly their principles, and co-ordinate the services.

Integration policy should be planned within an *administrative framework*. This presents a problem. In effect one waits for the administration to put into place the new perspectives. But in most of our countries an administration which manages special education, and which is solely responsible for this sector, is part of the whole problem. This in fact creates an internal resistance to change. One can also pose the question of how extensive is a central administration's power for making decisions. In other words, "At what levels are decisions made?" Clearly, in the field of integration, decisions should be taken at a local level, where one finds the key workers.

Factors that concern the key workers

The *educational politics* are slightly different in each school and its educational community. The headteacher will have a central role in determining these politics. All the decisions about integration should be made on the bases of clear information, of discussion, and of involvement of the whole team in the decision. The need for continuous whole school staff training on issues relating to integration naturally follows from this proposition.

The task and the development of the role of the *teachers* are other fundamental factors. The teachers are the levers for all integration. The principal responsibility rests on them. It is necessary to promote their knowledge, their understanding and their attitudes towards stimulating and organising successful individual and group teaching approaches in heterogeneous classes.

Therefore it is necessary to understand the ways in which children learn. Personal motivation, reflected by active involvement, is the catalyst in all learning processes. So the teacher needs, above all, to create an environment that is favourable to learning. In such a climate the essential role of a teacher is not simply to deliver the lessons but to initiate and to organise the learning processes, either individual or group. It is desirable to adopt a teaching approach that motivates the pupils; a teaching approach that concerns the learning rather than the teaching. It is evident that the necessary skills for undertaking such an approach need to be developed through staff training at all levels.

Above all, it is necessary to reinforce the position of *parents*. In practice this can be achieved through providing them with full and accurate information, in a spirit of true partnership, respecting the decision that they have to make and for which they have responsibility. To achieve this it necessary to demystify the role and the position of the specialists.

In order to achieve the best form of integration it is necessary to appraise parents of their own role. Integration is not necessarily the easiest route. One needs to take under consideration some parent's expectations, which may be too high. In that case it is desirable to clarify their expectations. Finally one should not disregard the questions, opinions and suggestions of parents of pupils without disabilities in the same classroom. Their views about integration need to be taken into account.

One must also consider the contribution that *specialists* and the various *support services* can make to successful integration. It is necessary to consider the various skills and the support that they can offer, but above all one should consider the relationship that they establish with those who hold the central responsibility for the child: *i.e.* the parents and the teachers.

In the context of integration the concept of support has changed completely. The aim is no longer only one of "treatment", but of supporting the teachers and the team. The main responsibility of the specialists is not one of problem-solving. In other words, the role of the specialist is not to resolve the problem, but to empower those with the central responsibility to find a solution themselves.

In countries where special teaching is delivered mainly in autonomous special schools, one must regard the possible contribution and eventually the support of these institutions within a policy that is aimed at integration.

Factors related to teaching

The choice of the *curriculum*, using the widest definition of the word, is fundamental for successful integration. The aim should be for all individual pupils to have curriculum access, so as the rest of their class, without a-priori restrictions. Specifically it is necessary to differentiate and/or to adapt the curriculum in recognition of each individual pupil's abilities. An important principle is to maintain an appropriate balance, between the pupil's entitlement to a broad curriculum and an appropriate preparation for an independent life. In this respect one should ask if a restricting diet of so called "basic skills", which have to be achieved by all the pupils in the school, creates an obstacle preventing integration for pupils, who because of their abilities will not be able to achieve these skills.

At the classroom level the primary focus is the ability to organise the delivery of the curriculum recognising *pupils' different learning styles*. Integration does not have a chance of being successful if the teaching approach is "didactic".

The most effective teaching approaches in integrated settings depend above all on creating situations conducive for learning. For example, the organisation of "work-units", planned across the whole school, or across a number of classes, is particularly effective. These will allow the pupils to work in a variety of groupings led by a coherent educational team in which every one has a clearly defined role.

It is important to address the question of *assessment*. The foundations of a real individualised special education approach, are built on the skills of those involved to assess and identify the needs of the pupils how they will perform and what their achievements will be. Formative assessment is a continuous process. It is achieved by the teachers looking for answers to the questions "What?" and "How?" These questions are far more important than the traditional approach to assessment. This traditional approach usually focuses on the question "Where?", and in many cases this easily takes away the responsibility from the key workers.

Conclusion

I wish to conclude by focusing on the principal player, the child. One should not categorise children just by labelling them. Each child has the right to be considered as a unique human being, called by their name, like you and I, a name that expresses their value and all their strengths and abilities.

Part III

ORGANISATION

CHAPTER 10

SUPPORTING THE CLASSROOM TEACHER IN NEW BRUNSWICK

by

Darlene Perner

Introduction

As part of the OECD/CERI study *Active Life for Disabled Youth -- Integration in the School*, integration was reviewed in three schools (elementary, junior high and senior high) within School District 12 in the Province of New Brunswick, Canada. The results were reported for the second phase of the *Integration in the School* project (Perner, 1993). The findings of this review indicated that an important component for successful integration/inclusion was in providing a variety of supports to classroom teachers. In particular, three supports for teachers were identified as being extremely beneficial to the classroom teachers. They are: the collaborative consultant (method and resource teacher), multi-level instruction, and the problem solving team. These three supports for classroom teachers are described in detail following the section on background information.

Background on integration in New Brunswick

In this section, New Brunswick's policy on integration is summarised and background information on School District 12 in Woodstock, New Brunswick is provided.

In 1986, the Province of New Brunswick passed legislation that requires the placement of exceptional students in regular schools and classes. Exceptional students have the right to access all educational programs and services and to be included in regular classes (Perner, 1993). In 1994, the New Brunswick Department of Education and school districts expanded on the provincial integration guidelines (Province of New Brunswick, 1988). They developed a set of beliefs, principles and indicators "that are considered to be the foundation of an inclusive education policy" (Perner and Porter, 1996).

Since 1985, School District 12 in Woodstock, New Brunswick have expanded their program and service delivery model for exceptional students from integration to inclusion. They have reached their initial goal of having all students attend community schools in age appropriate, regular classes. "There are no special schools or classes for exceptional students in this school district. The types and severity of disabilities vary in each school and are dependent on what natural proportion occurs within the community" (Perner, 1993, p. 3). Currently, those in School District 12 are working on having all students participate in instructional activities with their peers in regular classes.

School District 12 was selected for study in the OECD/CERI *Active Life for Disabled Youth -- Integration in the School* project because this district has had "many years of experience with integrating exceptional students in regular classes and has a strong commitment to the philosophy of integration" (Perner, 1993, p. 5). In 1992, school staff, parents and students from three schools in School District 12 were interviewed. The results of the interviews were used to identify successes and challenges with integrating exceptional students in regular classes. Based on the experiences of School District 12, several practices were identified that helped to support classroom teachers with integrating exceptional students.

Supports for teachers

In schools and in inclusive education classes, it is teachers who have the most significant impact on students. A positive influence occurs when teachers have supports that facilitate working closely with other teachers and with their students (National Center on Educational Restructuring and Inclusion, 1994; Sapon-Shevin in O'Neil, 1994; Crawford and Porter, 1992; Perner, 1991).

For the most part, students actively participate in regular class instruction with their peers in School District 12. This is mainly because classroom teachers seek out and are offered a variety of supports that foster and enhance inclusive schools.

In School District 12, support for classroom teachers is a major component for helping students to access the curriculum. In particular, three supports, consistently, have been identified by staff and parents involved in the integration process. They are:

1. the collaborative consultant (method and resource teacher);
2. multi-level instruction; and
3. the problem solving team.

These primary supports to classroom teachers are described below.

Collaborative consultant

With the onset of integration, one of the major changes in special education services has been the movement from the special class and resource room models to a collaborative consultation model. In this model, the consulting teacher (formerly the "special educator"), who in New Brunswick primarily is called the method and resource teacher, confers and collaborates with classroom teachers, parents and other support personnel and agencies to help include exceptional students in the regular classroom and ensure successful learning.

This approach emphasises that the knowledge and skills of all teachers (the method and resource teacher and classroom teachers) must be used in a collaborative manner. It is essential for method and resource teachers to be seen as colleagues who can assist teachers in finding workable strategies to help students access the curriculum. They should not be seen as "experts" who take responsibility for specific children and the difficulties that ensue (Collicott and Porter, 1992).

The collaborative consultation model has allowed for a smooth transfer of responsibility to the regular education teacher and system. Jerome Lynch (1993) from the United States supports this by stating, "We have learned that pulling teachers into the classroom is better than pulling students out."

Method and resource teachers are experienced classroom teachers who have additional training in a variety of areas. Their duties (as identified by the method and resource teachers in School District 12) can be categorised within four areas: collaboration; instruction; teacher support; other functions (Porter, 1991).

Collaboration includes working in a support role with teachers, parents, administrators, teacher assistants, students and community agencies "to establish programs or develop approaches to solve problems encountered by both students and teachers" (Porter and Collicott, 1992, p. 194). Observing and monitoring in class situations and assisting in the transition of students from class to class, and to schools and work are part of this collaborative process.

Instruction consists of the method and resource teacher either teaching the regular class while the classroom teacher works with an exceptional student; or, the method and resource teacher teaching individuals or small groups within and/or outside of the regular classroom.

In School District 12 many of the teachers have had experience both as method and resource teachers and as regular classroom teachers. Consequently, the method and resource teachers, experientially, are able to teach a variety of regular classes for specified periods of instruction. As well, the classroom teachers are able to provide individualised instruction to exceptional students within their class. For example, one of the classroom teachers interviewed in School District 12 had been a method and resource teacher for a number of years at the junior high school. Recently, she returned to regular class teaching. The new junior high school method and resource teacher supported this classroom teacher by teaching language arts to her class. While the method and resource teacher taught this regular class, the classroom teacher worked very intensely instructing a fourteen year old student with autism named Robert. The following is a paraphrase of what the regular class teacher said about having the direct support of the method and resource teacher (Dickinson, 1993).

> *Now I understand why classroom teachers appreciated my assistance when I taught their classes so that they could work with an exceptional student. How can a regular classroom teacher be expected to include an exceptional student like Robert without first knowing him and working with him on an individual basis?*

> *As I get to know Robert, I learn how to adapt the curriculum, what questions to ask him, what his strengths are for co-operative learning groups, and how to include him in all class activities. Without these opportunities with Robert, he would be in my class but excluded from most class activities.*

Teacher support includes functions such as processing referrals, assessing students, planning programs, planning and implementing volunteer and peer group programs, adapting curriculum, modelling teaching strategies, and preparing materials for classroom teachers. The focus of both classroom teachers and method and resource teachers is to collaborate on ways to include exceptional students in regular classroom instruction and activities.

Other functions of the method and resource teachers include school supervision duties, and professional development. In School District 12, professional development is offered to the method and resource teachers every two weeks.

Many of the classroom teachers interviewed for the OECD/CERI *Active Life for Disabled Youth -- Integration in the School* project indicated that the method and resource teacher was their primary support. The method and resource teachers' role in School District 12 has provided the main structure for the integration of exceptional children and the inclusion of all students in the regular class.

Multi-level instruction

The second major support to classroom teachers is multi-level instruction. Classroom teachers are not able to spend a great amount of time working individually with students. They must focus on accommodating exceptional students' instruction with other students (Campbell *et al.,* 1988).

Multi-level instruction is a strategy adapted by Stone and Collicott (Collicott, 1991, Campbell *et al.,* 1988) from the works of Schulz and Tumbull (1984). Multi-level instruction allows for planning and implementing one main lesson instead of a number of different lessons within a single class. The use of this strategy has been successful in involving, exceptional students, every student, at his or her own level in regular class lessons and activities.

The underlying question the teacher asks when planning and implementing an instructional activity for the class is "How can I include the exceptional student in this lesson?" To do this, it is important for the teacher to include various teaching and leaning techniques such as providing opportunities for students to have choices in how they will learn and practice skills, and how they will be evaluated.

There are four planning steps for developing instructional lessons and units within the multi-level instruction process. The multi-level instruction planning process consists of:

- identifying the underlying concepts to be taught;
- determining the method of presentation;
- establishing the method of practice and performance; and
- deciding on the method of evaluation. (Campbell *et al.,* 1988, pp. 17-18).

In multi-level instruction, the teacher starts with identifying the underlying concepts to be taught within a unit or a particular lesson. Even though students may have different objectives, the concept should be one that is shared by students. For example, if students who are 13 to 15 years old are studying the novel or short story, some of the underlying concepts to be taught may be character, plot, setting, and theme (Campbell *et al.,* 1988).

The next two steps of the multi-level instruction process are determining the method of presentation, and the method of performance and practice. These methods may include considering variations in teacher style, student learning style, preferred mode of presentation or performance, questioning techniques, level of thinking, and level of participation.

Students may partially participate in an activity by being paired with another student or doing only a segment of the activity based on their skill level. For example, one student may make a short presentation based on personal experience; whereas others in the class, may be doing longer presentations based on research (Collicott, 1991).

The key here is to allow for a variety of skill levels and a variety of ways to teach and give students choices which show that they understand the concept being taught. For example, if the concept of setting is being taught, then both methods of presentation and performance for lessons might include:

1. draw or find a picture to depict a described setting;
2. discuss home setting;
3. find a picture similar to one's home setting;
4. describe a setting of a television program or rock video;
5. construct a diorama of a setting to match a story; and
6. construct a setting for a school play or event (Perner and Stone, in press).

The fourth step in the multi-level instruction process is providing a variety of methods to evaluate whether each student has teamed the underlying concept being taught. For example, assignments used for evaluating the concept of settings might consist of oral presentations, illustrations, and the creation of settings (Perner and Porter, in press). "The point is that the teacher is not measuring writing or oral skills but whether the concept, in this case, setting is understood" (Perner and Stone, in progress).

In summary, multi-level instruction is a means to help teachers develop lessons that allow all students to participate in class instruction. The teachers interviewed in School District 12 indicated that multi-level instruction takes time and planning but they felt their exceptional students were participating and learning important concepts within the regular class.

Problem solving team

The third teacher support is the problem solving team. The problem solving team consists of a group of teachers who give support to each other by making suggestions focused on a specific problem. It provides opportunities for teachers to collaborate, to pool their resources, and to identify innovative ways to solve their problems related to the instruction and inclusion of students within the regular class.

Problem solving proceeds through an orderly sequence of steps. It starts with the "designation of the problem, to the development and implementation of a plan to resolve it, to evaluation of progress, to monitoring" (Porter *et al.*, 1991, p. 219). The model used in School District 12 was adapted by Porter *et al.* (1991) from Chalfant *et al.* (1979).

A facilitator, usually the school method and resource teacher, conducts the thirty minute problem solving team meeting. This time limit is strictly adhered to. The facilitator keeps team members on task by proceeding through an orderly set of stages to come up with possible solutions.

The process begins with a brief statement of the problem. Then, team members ask the teacher questions to help clarify the problem. For example, typical questions as identified by Porter *et al.* (1991) might be:

1. You find that Susan is aggressive toward other children. Can you give some specific examples of her aggressive behaviour?
2. What do you do when Joe does complete his homework?
3. In what subject area(s) is William succeeding? (p. 226)

After clarifying the problem, team members suggest possible solutions. These are brief and like the questions for clarification are done in a round-table fashion. Everyone takes a turn or turns in an orderly and equitable manner.

Consultation does not end with this problem solving team meeting but many possible solutions are elicited for the teacher. It is the responsibility of the teacher to select possible solutions to try. The teacher in collaboration with the method and resource teacher and others so designated are responsible for the resolution plan, its implementation and monitoring. The team may meet again for progress reports and/or to assist with changes in strategy.

The problem solving team process helps classroom teachers to feel enabled and supported by their colleagues. It provides an opportunity for teachers to collaborate, share ideas, help each other and make changes, changes that directly have an impact on students.

Summary

Three types of supports available to the classroom teachers involved in integration/inclusion have been described. School District 12 provide many other types of support to teachers besides the collaborative consultant (method and resource teacher), multi-level instruction, and the problem solving team. These include access to: the school district student services team; teacher assistants; a student services school team; parent involvement; and professional development focused on opportunities for meeting, planning and consultation, and on inclusive strategies such as co-operative learning, multi-level instruction, whole language, and activity-based learning.

When interviewing, teachers for the OECD/CERI project, however, it was made clear that:

1. teachers need supports so that students can access the curriculum within the regular class; and
2. classroom teachers prefer using specific supports and resources based on their own and their students' abilities and needs.

For example, some teachers favoured consultation time with the method and resource teacher or with the problem solving team. Other teachers felt they needed professional development or a teacher assistant. Even though three supports for teachers were identified, a variety of supports and teacher preferences for these supports need to be considered when helping students to access the curriculum in schools with integration or inclusion.

CHAPTER 11

INFLUENCES OF NATIONAL POLICIES ON CLASSROOM TEACHING AND CURRICULUM ACCESS IN ENGLAND

by

Klaus Wedell

Professor Marchesi, in his paper, identifies four main ways in which thinking about children and young people with special educational needs (SENs) should influence countries' educational policies. He rightly points out that these are ways in which policies need to be developed, if pupils with SENs are in fact to be given access to the curriculum.

In this paper, I would like to make a few points which deal with the issue of curriculum access at the level of general educational policies, and at the level of the individual teacher's work with pupils. I will make the points in the context of educational policy in England, since these illustrate some of the problems which may arise.

The impact of general educational policies

The main legislation about SENs in England was the 1981 Act, which has since been incorporated into the 1993 Act (Department for Education, 1993). The definition of SENs in the legislation was based on the acknowledgement that SENs were the outcome of interaction between the strengths and needs of the pupil and the resources and deficiencies in the pupil's environment - including the educational context. Such a view of pupils' SENs recognises that they occur in a continuum of degree, and so raises the question how educational provision can be organised to match this continuum.

As Professor Marchesi mentions, in considering this problem one has first of all to consider the conditions which prevail in ordinary schools. What is the range of SENs which an ordinary school can meet in its pupils? Professor Marchesi points out that an equally important question is whether schools regard it as their responsibility to respond to the individual needs of their pupils -- in other words, it is a question of attitudes. However, it immediately becomes evident that the extent to which schools and individual teachers can put positive attitudes into practice, depends on the practical support afforded in education systems.

Because of the financial constraints which are affecting most countries, there is a concern that special educational support should be cost-effective. Indeed, the legislation made integration conditional on "the effective use of resources". Since SENs occur across a range of severity, they have to be met with a corresponding range of expertise and specialised provision. It would not be cost-effective for all schools to offer the full range of provision from their own resources, and so in most countries, economy of scale is achieved by organising more specialist provision at levels above the individual school. Research which we have recently carried out (Lunt *et al.*, 1994), shows that one way in which economy of scale can be organised, is through collaboration between schools. We have studied "clusters" of schools which collaborate in sharing specialist staff and other resources to meet the range of the SENs of their pupils. Sometimes these clusters are formed on the initiative of individual schools, but more frequently the Local Education Authority (LEA) has encouraged such collaboration, by delegating to the clusters both the resources and the decisions about how these should be allocated among schools.

Even when some economies of scale above the level of the school can be achieved by collaboration between schools, provision for the more severe and low incidence SENs has to be organised at a higher level. In England, this organisation has, until recently, been the function of the LEA, which has been responsible for establishing a coherent system of support within their areas. Such support has consisted of special schools and units in ordinary schools, and by teams of specialist teachers supporting ordinary schools.

New legislation enacted from 1988 onwards was aimed at increasing the autonomy -- and correspondingly the accountability -- of individual schools and reducing the co-ordinating responsibility of LEAs. The aim was to introduce a "market economy" into education. In order to achieve this, the government produced a method of assessing the achievement of pupils, by introducing a prescribed National Curriculum (NC). This would allow parents to compare schools on the average level of achievement of their pupils. It was assumed that schools with higher achievement would attract more pupils, and so the new policy was aimed at funding schools according to the numbers of pupils they could attract.

The way in which these policies have worked out, provides an interesting illustration of how the general organisation of education can affect schools' capacity to meet their pupils' SENs. It also indicates that even apparently positive aspects of policies can have paradoxical effects. Two examples can be cited.

The introduction of a NC has, in principle, been welcomed by teachers. Potentially it offered them a common framework which enabled them to plan their teaching and to monitor individual pupils' progress across the whole range of achievement. The NC was aimed at accommodating the majority of pupils with SENs within its framework. Unfortunately however, the NC was focused on ten circumscribed subjects covering the age range from five to sixteen, and initially was linked to prescriptive "programmes of study" and forms of assessment. On both these counts, it was difficult to apply the curriculum across the range of pupils' SENs. Furthermore, the prescriptiveness of the NC and its assessment gave teachers an inordinate workload, and also made them feel de-skilled and demoralised, because it took away the autonomy which they had previously exercised in responding to pupils' individual needs. These potential problems had, of course, been pointed out when the legislation was originally proposed, and in recent years extensive changes have been introduced towards redressing them.

Another example of the paradoxical effects of policies is illustrated by the aspects of the legislation which required that LEAs should devolve to schools a very much larger proportion of the funds needed to run them. The aim was that this would allow schools to focus their expenditure more closely on their particular needs. From the point of view of schools' meeting their responsibilities to pupils with SENs, this would seem a very positive policy. However, as was already mentioned above, the allocation of funds to schools was based on pupil numbers, which in turn, forced the schools to compete for pupils. Since this competition was intended to be based on the average level of pupils' achievement, it became more difficult for schools to give priority to supporting pupils with

SENs, because these were unlikely to make a contribution to raising the average achievement. For example, the proportion of pupils leaving schools without a single grade at G or above in the General Certificate of Secondary Education has risen from 7 per cent to 8.1 per cent over the two years to 1995 (Hackett and Passmore, 1995). At the same time, because LEAs were required to devolve more of their funds to schools, LEAs themselves had fewer funds to provide support to schools to meet their pupils' SENs. There was also a significant increase in the proportion of pupils whose SENs schools claimed they could not meet (Evans and Lunt, 1994).

These two examples of educational policy provide rather stark illustrations of how individual schools' ability to offer their pupils access to curriculum can be affected.

Preparing teachers to ensure curricular access to pupils with SENs

Professor Marchesi also mentions that access to the curriculum has to be facilitated through training which supports the teacher in the classroom to carry out this task. Providing access involves teachers and their schools in considering how the education provided generally to pupils can allow for a flexible response to individual pupils' needs. However, beyond this, teachers also need a strategy both for deciding when it is necessary to focus more specifically on individual pupils' SENs, and also when to call in help from others. Partly as a result of concern expressed about the legislation mentioned in the previous section, a Code of Practice for identifying and meeting pupils' SENs was established following the 1993 Act (Department for Education, 1994). A major part of the Code is concerned with such a strategy. At the Institute of Education, London University, we have been looking at how such a strategy can be included in the training of teachers (Wedell, 1995).

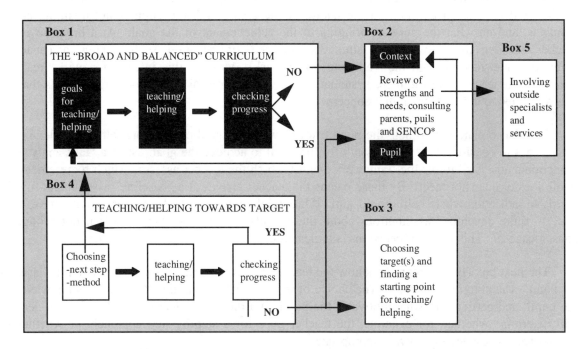

* SENCO: Special educational needs co-ordinator: a teacher in the school who has particular responsibility for co-ordinating teachers and work for children with SENs.

The strategy is illustrated in the following diagram. It focuses on helping teachers become aware of the decisions they make in responding to individual pupils' needs, and is based on discussions with experienced teachers on our advanced courses.

There has been much discussion of the role of the teacher as a "reflective practitioner". Our work on teacher decision making has been directed at trying to understand what is actually involved in this "reflection" as it relates to pupils with SENs. It assumes that the teacher is someone who is in a position to make decisions about facilitating pupils' access to the curriculum. It implies that teachers are given the responsibility for making decisions, and that they have the autonomy and understanding to do so. It also means that teachers need to have the time to think about their strategies. As mentioned in the previous section, the context in which teachers are expected to carry out their tasks may actually prevent them from doing so, even if they want to.

Box 1 in the top left hand part of the diagram represents the teacher's normal sequence of decisions in the classroom. The teacher moves through successive goals, and evaluates the pupils' progress. The goals may refer to curriculum subjects, or to the less specific aspects of the broader curriculum such as pupils' behaviour or work approaches. When the teacher notices that the pupil is not responding to her usual approaches, she is making a decision in relation to objective or subjective norms -- an "assessment" in the usual terminology. However, the strategy makes it clear that while this is the point where the teacher infers *that* there is a "problem", the line of enquiry then has to switch to looking at *why* there is a problem, in other words, an enquiry about causation.

Box 2 refers to this stage. The initial query relates to whether the "problem" lies with the teacher's approach, or with the pupil, or with both. For example, if the majority of pupils are not making the expected progress, then the "problem" is more likely to apply to the teacher's approach or the curriculum offered than to the individual pupil's difficulty. If the converse is the case, then the teacher will have to focus more on the nature of the goal which the pupil is not attaining and its demands, and on what the pupil is bringing to the achievement of the goal. At a broad level, the teacher considers the more obvious strengths and needs of the pupil, such as physical capacities, levels of understanding, and motivation to do the task. Most of this information will already be known to the teacher, but the more systematic analysis may reveal other more urgent goals than the one which led to the teacher's initial concern.

In order to plan how to help the pupil towards whatever goal or goals are felt to be relevant, the teacher has to consider what is necessary for the pupil to achieve the goal. Such a "task analysis" or "functional analysis" forms the framework against which the teacher assesses which requirements the pupil does or does not meet. By these means the teacher arrives at a "baseline" assessment, in other words an indication where help should start. (One should note that, while teachers usually have -- and apply -- quite developed assumptions about these kinds of analyses, they are often not brought to consciousness). This series of decisions is indicated in Box 3.

The next box (Box 4) represents how the teacher sets about teaching to the next step towards the goal and evaluating the outcome. The choice of method will be based on the teacher's knowledge of the pupil, and particularly what motivates the pupil, and the pupil's learning style. Such a decision will determine whether, for example, the teacher goes for a step-by-step approach, or whether the teacher feels a broader approach is appropriate.

The feedback arrows in the diagram indicate that these decisions in the successive boxes form progressive cycles. Both success in helping the pupil to succeed -- and failure, may lead the teacher back to earlier boxes. In these successive cycles, the teacher is learning about the pupil, and is learning how to see the problem through the pupil's eyes. One of the most important sources of information will be the pupil, who should be consulted as much as possible all through the strategy. The same applies to the pupil's parents who should be consulted from the initial stages.

If the cycle of modifying the teaching approach leads to the pupil regaining progress, the pupil will be reincorporated within the teacher's usual teaching approaches. The fact that the additional intervention approach is located in the diagram parallel to the normal teaching process is intended to indicate that the decision making sequences illustrated so far are not regarded as separate from the overall teaching activity. However, if the teacher's more specific approaches are not helping the pupil to regain progress, there will be a need to consider whether the goal is really appropriate for the pupil, and/or whether the pupil has needs which the teacher has not fully understood. At this point (see Box 5), the arrows in the model indicate that the teacher will wish to consult others who can help with information relevant to clarifying these decisions such as specialists within the school or outside it -- for example special needs advisory teachers, educational psychologists or speech therapists. The questions to them will involve ideas about the nature of the pupil's needs, and ideas about approaches which can be tried. The evaluation of the outcomes of the ensuing approaches will themselves be used as further information about the nature of the "problem". The diagram indicates that these investigations may still lead to new conclusions about the relevance of "within-child" and "environmental" factors.

The above account of the decision sequences surrounding the ways in which pupils' SENs may be identified and met indicate the level of skills, knowledge and understanding which training needs to offer teachers if they are to make their contribution to accessing the curriculum for pupils. This kind of strategy is frequently implied in much of what is offered during the professional preparation of teachers, but it is rarely made explicit. Similarly, most gifted teachers follow these lines in any case. However, unless the decision making is made explicit and intentional, teachers do not learn from their experience, and they cannot use their knowledge to communicate with others -- including the pupil. If teachers are to succeed in providing access to the curriculum, this kind of content has to be included in their training.

I have tried to indicate some of the micro -- as well as the macro -- considerations which determine whether teachers are able to make the curriculum accessible to pupils. I very much agree with Professor Marchesi's thesis, that the issue has to be addressed at both these levels, if schools are to be places where the necessary flexibility in approach can be achieved.

CHAPTER 12

A NATIONAL STRATEGY FOR ENHANCING ACCESS
TO THE CURRICULUM IN FRANCE

by
Patrice Couteret

Introduction

This paper concerning access to the curriculum in France starts from the same observations as those mentioned by Professor Marchesi in his paper dealing with the conditions for satisfactory integration. Here the emphasis is on "integrating" children with special needs nationally, according to an accepted and coherent conception, and in linking them locally in an adapted way, from a "strategic" viewpoint, through the writing of "individualised projects". It must be pointed out that these "projets" do not correspond to the general definition of "curriculum" used in this collection of papers. In France, for a proper understanding, "projets", "school programmes" and "curriculum" must be regarded as specific terms referring to different things.

A survey of the French system

To describe "access to the curriculum", for young people in need of special education in France, five factors must be considered.

1) France, traditionally a largely centralised country, started a large decentralisation movement following laws passed in 1982 and 1983. Furthermore, the principle of "subsidiarity" advocated by the European Union has been officially annexed by the French administration and by the Local and State administrations through the Law of the 6 February 1992. This trend was introduced into the education system by the Orientation Law of 1989 and other subsequent laws. This same law, in principle, has contributed to local initiatives following precise national objectives. By the year 2000, the plan is for 100 per cent of an age group to leave the education system with a level V (CAP level: Professional Aptitude Certificate [*Certificat d'Aptitude Professionnelle*]) and 80 per cent with a level IV (*Baccalauréat*). Presented from an expert's viewpoint the basic idea is to face up to the political and socio-economic requirements for the next century, which would make it necessary to improve the general scholastic level for French citizens and ensure a minimum qualification for all.

It is clear, that these goals are in line with the recent European Community's white book "Growth, Competitiveness and Employment", but apparently contradictory to the adopted "mixed strategy" -- and here is a major source of difficulty. In France, this mixed strategy requires a distinction to be made between local autonomy, seen as necessary for the relevance and individualisation of local action plans, and a global understanding determined through national objectives.

Within this context the functional integration of handicapped students is achieved through the preparation of "projets". These are reports written by those involved in local planning. They are individualised but based on consensual agreement of those involved, including the disabled pupil. In addition to this "projet" others will also be involved. For example, in the case of a physically disabled child there will be a pedagogic "projet". All of these "projets" will be prepared in consideration of the other "projets", leading to a coherent programme of locally planned and implemented action in line with National Legislation. The professionals who have prepared these written "projets" are responsible first to themselves and second to those further up in the hierarchy who must confirm that the "projets" meet national objectives. But according to the principle of subsidiarity, particularly effective and/or innovative "projets" can be given additional resources. Finally, the "strategy" allows for different partners to be brought together in a clearly described framework to develop "Integration agreements". These may be between a school which has enrolled a disabled pupil and for example a special school, parents or local support networks, and eventually businesses concerned with vocational training, and other higher levels of the national education system.

After many years of working with this approach it has become clear that the regulation and guidance of the system is dependent on detailed diagnostics and ordered plans of action at all levels of the system. Research and the development of relevant evaluations at local and national levels are the cornerstones of the effective development of the plan which also benefits, from experience rooted in France's history.

2) The French tradition of centralisation had led to the same national curriculum from *nursery school* (3 years olds) to *secondary school* (18 year olds). Therefore, for the professionals within the education system, the term "curriculum" originally and specifically refers to the national curriculum. The latest revisions pertaining to the above quoted objectives go back to 1985, and for 10 years now, the Ministry of Education has been creating, producing and distributing many documents to help teachers to assimilate the reforms, to put them into practice and work with a *reference system:* for example, the *"Evaluation Aids"* [*"Aides à l'évaluation"*] and the *"Student Booklets"* [*"Livrets de l'Elève"*] for primary, the "Complements" [*"Compléments"*] for secondary, the national evaluation to enter into CE2 (mid-primary) and in the 6th year (beginning of secondary), the *"diploma references"* [*"référentiels de diplômes"*] and the *"Competence Booklets"* [*"Livrets de compétence"*] for qualified training aimed towards adolescents with scholastic difficulties.

3) From what has been said so far, school integration may be considered as one aspect of social insertion (in the same way as professional qualification, personal independence and diversified social relationships are encouraged by the *Loi d'orientation* of 1989). This means that school integration (full time and individual integration in an ordinary school for a student in need of a special education) is regarded as a desirable but non-compulsory and/or centrally controlled aim, because it is the goal of social insertion in the long-term which determines the choice of education placement. This is especially true for teenagers and young adults (see the third case study described briefly later). It must also be understood that disabled and/or students with difficulties have the same rights and responsibilities as all other students, that is:

– they have the right to education and adapted measures in case of difficulties and to benefit from an Individualised Education Plan (IEP) which is developed with and by them and their parents and the professionals. This IEP determines the objectives in relation to the curriculum and examinations and the steps needed to achieve these goals as well as the most suitable type of provision (*e.g.* boarding with full-time integration; day hospital with part-time integration; full or part-time provision in a special class in a regular school).

– they must abide by the "school attendance" rules (their parents are informed about their "scholastic obligations"). They must keep up with the same curriculum and prepare for the same examinations, competitions and/or vocational certificates, and these normative evaluations are referenced to the same national standards (*e.g.* at the second cycle of primary education, at the 6th level and for the diploma). In principle, only the on-going formative and summative evaluations are adapted to the levels of the students' abilities.

4) In the French system, specialised teachers who already have a three year working experience as "ordinary" teachers follow a one year intensive training course in a specialised centre, for example, CNEFEI.[1] They are trained for a specific kind of difficulty (motor, visual, mental or learning difficulties), with educational content and method, and are familiarised with problems related to multidisciplinary work. They are qualified to take charge of specialised classes (either in private or state schools) or to be in charge of specialised support for integrating students. Their work to support integration complements that carried out by the school teachers, who integrate the student(s) with difficulties and/or disabilities in their classes. (There is generally only one type of disability per class). Training courses or information days on the problems they may encounter are organised for these mainstream teachers.

5) In France, rather than using the term "integration", it would probably be more accurate to speak of a "reduction of segregation". With the highly segregated situation that exists in France and, individual integration representing only 7 per cent of the population of declared disabled students in 1991, the country decided to make integration easier in all its forms. However, the implementation of the above principles (especially the individualisation of the "projets") should not be carried out in a rigid way, since the law assumes that the most adapted treatment centre for the child's difficulties should also be as close as possible to his home. The present trend is :

• a wider range of treatment centres: boarding or day-school, in a specialised school with or without partial integration, specialised classes within ordinary schools, specialised education services and home care, part-time or full-time individual integration, etc.; and,

• a distribution of the different reception centres, as homogeneously as possible, throughout the country.

In conclusion to these general considerations, it can be said that the development of diverse forms of integration over the years, has had the effect of redefining the work and practices of these establishments and specialised services.

Three significant examples

The first is of an eight year old boy with slight mental disability who would have been able to have been taught according to the curriculum of the second cycle. However, every day he went to a special class in a day-hospital far from his home, where he followed first cycle classes (which corresponded to nursery school). The professionals thought that he had developed sufficiently to be

---

1. CNEFEI: Centre national d'études et de formation pour l'enfance inadaptée.

able to be integrated into an ordinary class, and the special class teacher thought that in some subjects he had reached a level close to those required in the second cycle. With his parents' approval and a voluntary school teacher, they decided to integrate him in a school next to his home for three half-days a week using teaching materials adapted to his level of learning.

The second is of a five year old girl with a visual disability. Her level was assessed as being at the end of the first cycle and this allowed her to be integrated in a nursery school where she followed most of the "ordinary" classes. Moreover, different games and settings, adapted to children with visual disabilities, had been installed. Several times a week a specialised aide gives her some support in the subjects in which she has difficulties and proposes specific exercises for her to learn, for example in Braille.

The third is of a woman of 21 years of age with a motor disability. She had been fully integrated until the age of 18, after which she boarded in a specialised establishment, and had earned a Vocational Studies Certificate. After receiving this Certificate, and living 50 kilometres away from the establishment, she chose to continue in this establishment on a part-time basis in order to follow a relevant training leading to a qualification that would enable her to find employment in her region.

Conclusion

In conclusion, it is important to make two main points. According to the French "strategic" choices, "access to the curriculum" for young people in need of a special education, inevitably presents a paradox. The problems we meet deal mostly with the adapted social regulations, in other words, in guiding the implementation of the various "projets". On long term basis individualisation must be linked to overall coherence. This is rather intricate, but it may be understood by recognising that a young disabled person can be integrated. If the individualisation of the "projet" takes the child's difficulties into account, does that not mean that within the national context, they can live "like anybody else?"

The second point is more personal and is a rather epistemological reflection about our work. If we consider the principle of subsidiarity as being essential, the status of experts must be changed. In fact, in a highly centralised system (where local goals are determined centrally) the experts' or scientists' knowledge can appear as an almost absolute constraint on local decisions. In a decentralised system (where progress is locally determined, pragmatic and by agreement) the experts' knowledge although still necessary, acts only as an aid in decision making. In this case, experts become partners in local decision-making, instead of being the guarantors of central directives.

CHAPTER 13

PEDAGOGICAL, CURRICULAR AND CLASSROOM ORGANISATION IN ITALY

by

Lucia de Anna

Introduction

It is well known, that in Italy, children with disabilities have been enrolled and integrated in regular schools for more than twenty years. The milestones in the process through which the nation proceeded to implement this choice consist of a series of well-conceived and well-designed legislative and administrative measures, most recently the framework law 104 enacted in 1992, a presidential decree dated February 24, 1994, and the Ministry of Education's new rules on final examinations and grading (issued in March 1995 and applicable as of the current school year), which specify criteria to be used in evaluating pupils with disabilities. Over these twenty years, much effort has gone into trying to change the Italian school system and set new goals that reflect above all the need to shape whole human beings, in light of changes in educational practice that gave rise to a still-unresolved controversy between "theoretical" and "scientific" pedagogy.

In this process of revitalising the school system, much emphasis has been placed on diversity, construed in pedagogy too as a basic epistemological and operative category. Diversity has come to be seen in terms of enhancement and encouragement, and in education the goal is to design a pedagogical system that can give each pupil the chance to express and optimise his or her own individuality.

Educational science aims to identify the "specialness" of each pupil's multiple forms of intelligence, cognitive styles and learning strategies, ways of expression and communication; his or her personal, intellectual and emotional history; the uniqueness of each person's path through life. This approach creates new opportunities to motivate, guide and support each pupil's overall development.

Italy is in the midst of a transition to educational methods open to a multitude of languages, intelligences, logic's, cultures and interpretative hypotheses. The education of a child with disabilities cannot be reduced to a simple process of socialisation; its goal is to strengthen the capabilities he or she does have, to elicit and activate new ones to the extent possible, and to devise alternative routes to the common goal, the shaping of whole human beings. Creating such a "design for life" for a child with disabilities requires the efforts and skills of different specialists who can provide the ensemble of information needed to intervene in the learning process. These considerations are the outcome of the long and laborious process that led Italy to make the choice to integrate children with disabilities in regular schools.

It is important to recall that choice reversed a long and solid tradition of special schools going back to the nineteenth century. The pedagogical approach, however, took shape in the early years of this century, with the Romagnolis' work in Rome for the blind, Pendola's in Siena for the deaf, De Santis and Montesano's in Rome for children with psychological disabilities, and all of Montessori's intense activities, to mention just the most eminent names. The current status of the integration model that has been developed in Italy over the past few years can be considered in the light of this background information.

An integration model

Current integration policy in Italy was established by presidential decree in February 1994. The decree was criticised in many quarters because the inter-institutional relations and actions it provided for were considered overly complex. While the policy's procedures are mandatory nation-wide, they are rarely applied with the full participation of all the operators who are supposed to be involved. In reality, integration can be successful only by proceeding according to this scheme, though some aspects can doubtless be streamlined and the tasks of the various actors need to be better defined. The policy's successive procedures are described on a phase by phase basis in the following paragraphs and are represented in diagrammatic form at the end of this paper.

In Phase 1, *the case is reported*. This can be when the parents register their child for the first time and submit a medical diagnosis. Conversely, the school itself may notice a pupil's disability during the learning-teaching process and report it to specialists. In this case, parental authorisation is required.

With the report in hand, the school can assign the pupil a support teacher, special materials and aid, but still does not have all the information needed to understand the child fully. This requires a *functional diagnosis* describing his or her pathology, disabilities, capabilities and skills. This diagnosis must also state what can be done to enhance the child's capabilities and skills. In fact, it does not suffice to simply say, for instance, that the child has Down's syndrome. The examiner must define the pupil's level of mental inadequacy, difficulties in the area of abstract operations and understanding language, ability to relate, attention span, ability to memorise, space-time orientation, and so forth.

This diagnosis provides the initial input for a *dynamic-functional profile* prepared by the child's teachers jointly with social and health-care operators. According to article 12 of the framework law (no. 104/1992), the dynamic-functional profile should "indicate the pupil's physical, psychological, social and emotional characteristics, his or her disability-related learning difficulties and chances of recovery, and the capabilities that must be supported, elicited and gradually strengthened and developed consistently with the disabled person's own cultural choices". The profile is reviewed from time to time in order to determine the effects of the various actions taken and the influence of the school environment. The profile is termed "dynamic" because it is updated whenever the pupil is promoted from one level of schooling to the next, and periodically during high school.

The review process makes it possible to depart from an exclusively medical approach. For instance, a doctor might say that a child with spastic tetraparesis will never be able to lift himself out of a given position, but it sometimes happens that his teachers and physical therapists manage through skill and determination to achieve unanticipated results, raising the person to a higher level of functionality. In other words, a diagnosis can change over time. Drawing up a dynamic-functional profile requires a great deal of work, from observation of the pupil's behaviour to the preparation of special tests and questionnaires. Family participation is a must. The home environment must be examined in relation to the pupil's problems, with the aim of removing any obstacles to the disabled person's full enjoyment of the right to an education.

Next, *an individual education plan* is designed on the basis of all the information collected. Educational activities should be tailored to each pupil, in the sense of initially setting up teaching situations adapted to the differences that appear among the pupils, offering them diversified and easier learning conditions. Their starting points are then gradually modified with the aim of achieving the best final results for all. The factors in play are not only teaching actions but also psycho-pedagogical actions, from the observation of behaviour to planning and evaluation. In this sense, the individual education plan for a pupil with a disability is simply tailored to greater diversity.

In Italy, schooling programmes are defined at the national level, but school staff try to play down the notion of a programme imposed from outside by building teaching/learning strategies through the curriculum and choices of contents. Introducing the concept of a curriculum in educational planning thus requires a thorough understanding of school realities, accurate analyses and descriptions of educational goals, the production and use of more complex teaching materials, and repeated assessment of the curriculum itself.

The curriculum concept includes all the essential elements of the teaching process and is based primarily on criteria of flexibility, properly grounded choice, consideration of environmental circumstances and facts regarding the school itself, available resources, and, most important, the pupils' knowledge, skills and motivation. For pupils with disabilities, especially those with serious handicaps, the choice of curriculum is fundamental, and the options favour a functional type of curriculum rather than an instrumental one.

The Ministry's new rules define the criteria for evaluating the performance of pupils with disabilities according to the chosen curriculum. As a rule, pupils with physical and sensory disabilities are rated by the same standards as the others, but teachers may use special tools when learning levels cannot be determined through discourse or traditional written tests. Pupils with psychological disabilities are also subject to evaluation, because the process itself has educational value and stimulates the pupil.

At the end of each three- or four-month marking period and at the end of the school year, *the class council reviews the teachers' reports* on the learning levels the pupil has attained in regular classes and through extra-curricular and support activities, verifies the overall results in relation to the goals established in the individual education plan, and judges whether or to what degree those goals have been reached. If the class council finds that the pupil has reached learning levels that meet or are comparable to the goals set by the ministerial programs, it must evaluate the pupil by the same system applicable to all the others.

If the individual education plan was diversified in view of educational and training goals not based on the ministerial programs, in order to guarantee the pupil with a psychological disability (or, in exceptional cases, the pupil with a physical or sensory disability) his or her right to an education, the class council is required to grade the pupil's learning performance with reference solely to the individual education plan, not to the ministerial programs. (In such cases, the council must file a detailed report thereon). This type of grading has legal value only for the purposes of allowing pupils to continue their studies in order to attain the goals set in the individual education plan (IEP). These pupils may be promoted or held back, and their report cards must be marked with the following text: "These grades refer to the IEP, not to the ministerial programmes, and were assigned pursuant to art. 13, Ministerial Ordinance 80 dated 9 March 1995."

Pupils graded on this differentiated basis are not admitted to final examinations leading to high school diplomas. If the pupil is held back, the class council must lower the goals set in his or her individual education plan. Pupils with physical, psychological or sensory disabilities may enrol in the same grade or class up to three times. If the class council finds the next year that the pupil has attained learning levels comparable to the goals set in the ministerial programs, it must grade him or her in the regular way. In this case, the pupil is not required to pass tests on subjects studied during the prior year or years, because the council already has all the information it needs.

If the council intends to apply differentiated evaluation, it must first notify the pupil's family and set a date by which the family may give its formal consent thereto. If explicit consent is not forthcoming, the procedure is considered accepted. If the family explicitly withholds its consent, the pupil may not be considered to have a disability and must be evaluated in the same way as the others.

Pupils with psychological disabilities who are not admitted to final examinations leading to a high school diploma are allowed to repeat the last year of their course of study, or may ask the school to issue a certificate of attendance. Although this type of certificate has no legal effects, it can serve to admit the pupil to a vocational training course, pursuant to agreements between the Ministry of Education's provincial offices and regional governments.

PROCEDURES ESTABLISHED IN ITALY BY PRESIDENTIAL DECREE DATED 24 FEBRUARY 1994
(Direction and coordination of Local health Boards duties in respect of disabled children)

The Regional Governments are responsible for ensuring that Local Health Boards provide the medical and educational services to disabled children necessary to achieve the aims set forth in articles 12 and 13 of Law 104/1992. The Boards are required to prepare the following reports:

Functional diagnosis

Dynamic functional profile

REGIONAL ADMINISTRATIONS ARE RESPONSIBLE FOR ENSURING THAT THE INTEGRATION PROCESS IS CARRIED OUT PROPERLY

ACTORS	PHASES	ACTIONS

Specialist

Case reported to school

School principal or psychologist reports case to Local Health Board within 10 days after receiving case report.

Multidisciplinary unit comprising:
Medical specialist
Child psychologist
Rehabilitation therapist
Social workers

Functional Diagnosis

Acquisition of information:
a) Clinical
b) Psychological

a) Clinical information:
-Medical examination
-Previous medical documentation

b) Psychosocial information
- Registry office data
- Information from family

Multidisciplinary unit comprising:
Medical specialist
Child psychologist
Rehabilitation therapist
Social workers
Regular teachers
Specialised teachers
Child's parents

Dynamic Functional Profile (Assessment)

Analytic description (based on the functional diagnosis) of child's potential levels of response to present/possible relationships.

Evaluation results

Local Health Board physicians
Specialised teachers
Educational psychologists
Child' parents

Individual Educational Plan

Based on Fd and DFP, each unit member recommends appropriate steps. Their recommendations are used to prepare an overall educational plan.

Evaluation results

Contents

Balanced, integrated actions tailored to the disabled child over a specific period of time in order to guarantee his/her right to an education.

Regular teachers
Specialised teachers

Individual Educational Plan

Every 3 months if possible, operators verify the effects of the actions and the school environment on the disabled child.

Evaluation results

Contents

Factors making it possible to dertermine whether the actions are effectively geared to the child's capabilities at each level of learning and rehabilitation

Evaluation results

CHAPTER 14

INTEGRATION IN THE ORDINARY SCHOOL IN SWITZERLAND

by

Gérard Bless

The system of education in Switzerland

To date, the Swiss Confederation includes 26 cantons, which can be considered as rather autonomous states. Above all in the fields of education and cultural affairs, each canton is highly independent and self-responsible. The cantonal Ministries of Education are the highest authorities of the school administration. Thus, Switzerland does not have a central Ministry of Education and accordingly no general school system, but 26 different school organisations. In parts, they differ widely from one another, but they all have one basic condition in common: every child has to attend school from the age of 7 to 15 or 16 years. Children spend different lengths of time in primary education according to the canton (see diagram below). During the school year 1993/94, an average of 4.6 per cent of all pupils attended a class or a school with a special curriculum (*Bundesamt für Statistik*, 1994, p. 16). This percentage includes pupils with learning disabilities and/or behaviour disorders, who are mainly schooled in self-contained special classes. These classes are also part of the public school system, for which the cantonal Ministers of Education are responsible. Some of the pupils with speech disorders, hearing impairments, visual impairments, physical handicaps, severe behaviour disorders and/or mental retardation are taught in residential schools. These institutions are not directly subordinate to the cantonal Ministries of Education and they are largely subsidised by the Federal Disability Insurance.

For the better understanding of the following account, two facts are of importance:

- On the one hand, the Swiss school authority is extremely decentralised with its 26 Ministries of Education. Despite various efforts to reach a minimal co-ordination between the cantons, on the national level there are no legal regulations concerning the integration in ordinary schools. Therefore there are no official directions nor national concepts for the integration of children with disabilities, except for one recommendation, dating from 1985, which is hardly ever taken into account (*Schweizerische Konferenz der kantonalen Erziehungsdirektoren* 1995, pp. 101-102). In Switzerland, the cantonal Ministries of Education are clearly responsible for the integration of children with disabilities and on a cantonal level, an increasing tendency towards integration has been observed over the past few years. Several cantons strive to integrate special education into the ordinary system of education.

- On the other hand, the Federal Disability Insurance is of high importance for the development of integration in Switzerland. It has a mostly impeding influence on all integrative efforts, as it only subsidises the education of pupils with disabilities in special schools and classes. Thus the cantons, which for instance are responsible for the schooling and education of mentally handicapped children, are not interested in integrating these pupils, because their schooling in special institutions is largely subsidised by the Federal Disability Insurance. However, a few enactments of the Federal Disability Insurance allow an integrative pedagogic and therapeutic care for pupils who need speech therapy, psychomotor therapy or training in hearing and lip-reading.

The following diagram provides an overview of the Swiss system of education.

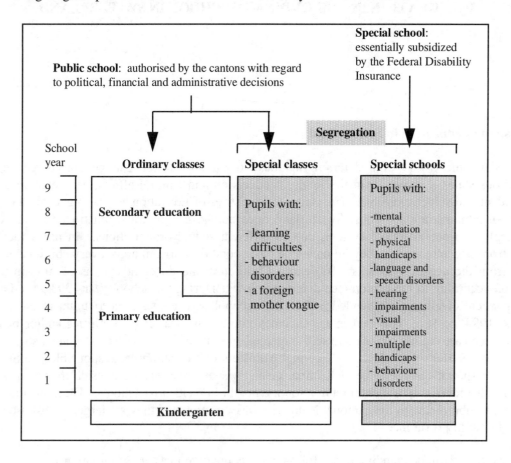

How has integration been realised up to now?

Integration is described as the common schooling and education of handicapped and non-handicapped pupils in ordinary classes of the public school system, with an adequate support for the children with special educational needs. This definition does not include the school settings which only practice a more or less close co-operation between special classes and ordinary classes, even if both types of classes are located under the same roof, which may allow regular interactions between handicapped and non-handicapped pupils. Real integration is characterised by common instruction of all pupils. Integration cannot be realised by a loose co-operation between ordinary and special classes, for instance for particular subjects, particular lessons or particular sporadically organised common projects. Such co-operation between ordinary and special classes is no essential step towards real integration in the true sense of the word, because it is no real reform of the school system. It only grants a kind of hospitality to the handicapped pupils, without really changing the ordinary school system towards an integrative school for all pupils.

Most of the pupils with special educational needs in ordinary classes are children with speech and language disorders. Speaking of this category of pupils, it would be more appropriate to talk about non-segregation instead of integration. Despite their special therapeutic needs, these pupils have never been systematically segregated. Only about 5 to 10 per cent of the children with speech and language disorders are referred to a special school. But most of the time, the speech and language impairments of these segregated pupils are not their initial problem; in addition they also suffer from behaviour disorders and/or learning difficulties. In Switzerland, pupils with particular as well as with complex speech and language disorders are not segregated because our public school system can provide a dense network of special logopedic support.

The most remarkable development towards mainstreaming can be observed in the field of learning difficulties. About 15 years ago, pupils with learning difficulties could remain in their ordinary class for the first time. Besides the instruction based on the regular curriculum they did get special assistance by a support teacher. At present, approximately 300 Swiss schools practice this kind of integration. About 8 to 12 per cent of all pupils with learning difficulties are integrated in ordinary classes. This seems to be quite a low quota, but with regard to Swiss standards it can be considered as a rather high proportion (Bless, 1995, pp. 61-64).

Pupils with a foreign mother tongue attend ordinary classes in most Swiss cantons. Usually they get special support for improving their knowledge of the standard school language. Several cantons with a high density of population run special classes for these pupils, but they aim at integrating them in ordinary classes as soon as possible. But despite these integrative tendencies, the statistics plainly show a growing number of pupils with a foreign mother tongue in special classes.

Pupils with physical handicaps and those with hearing and visual impairments are integrated on a small scale. Two preconditions are essential for their mainstream placement. On the one hand, these pupils have to be able to achieve the academic standard of their class without a differentiation of the regular curriculum. On the other hand, the schools have to be able to make available the necessary therapeutic support on their premises.

Despite the fact that attempts to realise integration in Switzerland, have been limited, several encouraging projects have been initiated lately. Some special schools have taken the offensive: they begin to provide support for pupils with special educational needs who attend ordinary schools. For example, the staff of a special school support several mentally handicapped children attending the kindergarten of their residential area. One special school for pupils with hearing and language impairments is transforming its division for the hearing impaired into a support and advice centre. They close down their special classes, integrate the pupils in ordinary classes and grant them a systematic regular support. These individual cases should not be overvalued but they can give signals for further attempts.

Looking back on the evolution of mainstreaming in Switzerland, we notice that integration depends on two conditions:

- *Integration must not cause any further expense.* As long as integrative measures do not cause any further expenditures, the cantons are willing to promote them. If integrative measures exceed the regular expense, the cantons do stop such efforts. For example the integration of pupils with learning difficulties does not cause any problems as the cantons finance both ordinary classes and special classes. Therefore, it does not matter in what classes these pupils are schooled. Pupils with speech and language impairments can be mainstreamed, because the Federal Disability Insurance will pay for their special support without having these pupils referred to a special school.

- *Integration must not disturb the regular schooling in the classroom.* As long as classroom instruction can be realised in its ordinary way, integration will be accepted. As soon as teachers have to individualise their lessons beyond a certain degree, integration does not have a good chance. For example, hardly any pupils with hearing impairments or additional severe learning difficulties will be found in ordinary classes, because integrating these children would ask for a high degree of differentiation and individualisation.

At this point we have to go back to the question: *Has integration in the ordinary school in Switzerland only slowed down or has it come to a stand-still?* If we take into consideration the number of integrated pupils, we can observe neither a slow-down nor a stand-still. If we consider the *categories* of pupils who are integrated into mainstream education, integration seems to have come to a stand-still, because many groups of handicapped children -- especially the mentally handicapped -- can only dream of integration. As long as the very special structures of financing those with disabilities in Switzerland are not fundamentally changed, true and real integration -- that means common education and schooling of *all pupils* -- will never be possible. Only a basic reorganisation of our financial system can open the way to a school reform which aims at integration in the true sense of the word.

The following factors do or may obstruct a further reorganisation of the Swiss system of education in favour of true integration. Probably these obstacles are not only a Swiss characteristic, but that they can be applied to various other countries, where they may have the same effects:

- A political system with 26 autonomous Ministries of Education for a total of 900 000 school-age children is not very flexible in order to reorganise the education system within a useful period.

- The political will to support integration is non-existent in Switzerland as a whole.

- Financial resources set a limit to integration. The structures of financing those with disabilities in Switzerland have been drawn up in view of segregation. They corroborate segregation and place at a disadvantage all the cantons which strive for an extensive integration.

- Unlike the advocates for integration, the special schools can rely on an efficient lobby. Most of the boards of directors of special schools can count on the honorary support of popular politicians and of other well-known personalities of regional or cantonal importance.

- Compared to Germany or Austria for instance, Switzerland does not have any significant parents' movement.

What can be done in favour of integration despite all the obstacles mentioned above? A reorganisation of the system of education towards a school for *all* children can only be realised if a clear strong political will in favour of integration can be established. On the one hand, this political will is a necessary precondition of a change of the Federal Disability Insurance such as to uncouple the financing of those with disabilities from their segregation in special schools and classes. On the other hand, a strong political will is needed not only to move the 26 school administrations in the same direction, but also to win as many special schools as possible to transform into support and advice centres in favour of integration. Probably in Switzerland this transformation will be a protracted affair. It will happen in small steps like the solution of many other factual issues on the political level. This policy of graduation implies a lot of small integrative projects, a high public presence with well-aimed specific information on integration, and persuasive argumentation face to face with politicians. A strong and efficient parents' movement would be of high benefit for such a concerted action.

CHAPTER 15

INCLUSION-PROMOTING FACTORS IN THE NORWEGIAN SCHOOLS

by

Ida Drage

Introduction

The Norwegian school system is based on several fundamental principles: equal educational opportunities for all, social and cultural solidarity, democratic decision-making at the school, and active participation at all levels.

These principles have led to a system of education that plays a very important role in Norwegian society, and is an essential factor for the further development of a modern welfare society based on democracy, solidarity and equality.

This paper focuses on primary and lower secondary education (the nine years of compulsory schooling in Norway).

One of the principles of Norway's educational policy is to keep primary and lower secondary pupils together in their own community. A comprehensive school for all pupils is an old idea, and after the 1975 amendment to the Primary and Lower Secondary Education Act of 1969, the inclusion principle has also applied to severely handicapped pupils, who were earlier often segregated in special schools. The Act clearly establishes that it is the local authority, the municipality, that is responsible for organising education for these pupils.

The principle, that special education should be provided in the local community is related to another fundamental goal: that Norwegian children should be able to complete their compulsory education without having to leave home. This, along with Norway's scattered rural population, makes it not only desirable, but also necessary, to integrate handicapped children into the ordinary school.

This educational policy makes it necessary to build up a system of consultants to advise the schools. Therefore the former schools of special education have recently been transformed into 20 national resource centres for special education. These centres, together with the local educational-psychological service, are there to help the municipalities and the schools to provide suitable education for children with special needs.

The structure of the educational system

The Norwegian system of education has four main levels:

- Primary and lower secondary education (comprehensive, compulsory education for pupils aged 7 to 16 years)
- Upper secondary education (students aged 16 to 19 years -- all adolescents in Norway are entitled to three years upper secondary education (can be extended to five for students with disabilities), consisting of academic, vocational or both academic and vocational subjects.
- Higher education at college or university.
- Adult education

The primary and lower secondary schools are administered by the municipality (the lowest level of local government) and the upper secondary schools by the county.

All "state" education is free. Before 1986 the government's allocations to the municipalities were earmarked for specific purposes. Since 1986, the municipalities have received a general grant, and are themselves responsible for distributing the funds between the different sectors, including the schools. If a child's needs cannot be met within the ordinary budget allocated to the school, then extra funds can be provided after assessment of the individual case by experts, after which the municipality decides how best to implement the recommended programmes of education. National standards are ensured through the legislation, which firmly establishes that pupils with disabilities are entitled to the same opportunities for education as other children. All decisions are made in close collaboration with the home.

The process of transforming the former national schools of special education into national centres for special education was started in 1992, and is still going on. The objective is a national system of support, to ensure that all children, young people and adults with special needs will be offered good, meaningful and well-organised education adapted to their own aptitudes and abilities, preferably in their own community.

Suitably adapted education

The general part of the new National Curriculum states that "the school shall have room for everybody, and teachers must therefore have an eye for each individual learner".

The Curriculum Guidelines for Compulsory Education in Norway state that suitably adapted education is a fundamental principle for all the teaching in the school. The question of handicapped children's right to education, and the scope and form of this education, is closely linked to assessment by experts. This is where the educational-psychological service and the national centres for special education come in. They can assist the municipalities, the schools and the teachers to prepare individual teaching programmes for these children, based on their learning abilities and special needs, and their parents' priorities. They also advise on how the specific programme should be implemented, and estimate what it will cost. The programmes should ensure education of the same quality as that provided for pupils without functional disorders. This implies that all subject syllabuses, and the associated teaching, must be adapted to the educational needs of each student.

The challenge when practising the integration ideology

All people have a basic need to interact with others. To be able to exist in a social context, have friends and feel appreciated for what one is and what one does, are extremely important for one's self-confidence, self-esteem and quality of life. Most people feel lonely and worthless if this need is not met, and their quality of life deteriorates.

When pupils with disabilities are educated in ordinary primary and secondary schools, everyone concerned has an obligation to satisfy not only their educational needs but, as far as possible, their social needs as well. Otherwise, it is impossible to talk about real integration, or a school for all. If the education for children with special needs ignores the social aspects, then they become socially isolated from the other pupils in the different grades. This may be the biggest challenge in Norway today when putting the principle of integration into practice.

Providing suitably adapted education for handicapped pupils in the ordinary schools is a continuous process, and the need for individualised education must be balanced against the need for social participation with other pupils. The main pitfall, to be avoided in our efforts to achieve integration, is to focus too strongly on individualised education in the different subjects and forget the social arena.

Educators and school politicians in Norway need to learn more about how to achieve the goals of an all-inclusive school. This means learning more about the factors that make the integration of pupils with special needs into the ordinary schools a success.

During the re-organisation of special education in Norway, a National Users' Forum (*i.e.* parents, and their various organisations) has been established, directly linked to the Ministry and run by the Norwegian Association of the Disabled. The intention is to guarantee that the standpoints of the various groups of people with disabilities are heard, through exchange of information and direct discussions with the Ministry, the national resource centre boards, the educational-psychological service, etc. The users consider it extremely important to create an inclusive atmosphere in the school and the classroom.

A case study demonstrating important factors for successful integration

Various studies have tried to identify factors that promote successful integration of pupils with disabilities into the ordinary school. Data from a case study (Nordhal and Overland 1993) conducted for the OECD Study on Integrating Students with Disabilities into Mainstream Schools are of interest.

The study covered two local schools, each with 200-300 pupils aged 7 to 12 years, 20-24 teachers, and 2-3 assistant teachers. At both, the handicapped pupils attend ordinary classes. Most of them are also educated in groups together with other handicapped pupils. The goal is full social integration. The schools have 19 handicapped pupils. For 16, the diagnosis is "severe learning disabilities", for two others "psychosocial problems", and for one "autism". All have general learning difficulties, and the main problem in the primary school is to help them to acquire the necessary basic knowledge, skills and social attitudes for a good quality of life.

All the pupils belong to an ordinary class, and the class teacher has the same responsibility for these pupils as for the rest of the class, even if they are taught in small groups, or even alone.

The two schools use the same model for individualising the subject syllabuses, and the educational goals often differ from pupil to pupil. There are three categories of educational goals, related to:

- situation in life;
- social role and self-confidence; and,
- knowledge, skills and ideals (attitudes).

Method of evaluation

The main question asked in the evaluation was the following: to what extent does the content of the educational programme and the organisation of the education influence the social integration of pupils with severe learning disabilities in the primary school?

A combination of quantitative and qualitative methods was used. The data and the interpretations are based on interviews with teachers and pupils, including handicapped pupils who were capable of answering the relevant questions, and on questionnaires and reports. All teachers in schools containing pupils with disabilities were each to write a report every month, assessing to what extent they had succeeded in their efforts to realise specific educational goals. Some of the conclusions are stated below.

Some conclusions

At both schools, the pupils without disabilities show an accepting attitude towards those with disabilities, and take the initiative for social contact.

While the pupils without disabilities accept those with disabilities to some degree, only a few of them are together with the pupils with disabilities after school hours.

The answers from the teachers confirm these two conclusions.

The pupils with disabilities experience a sense of belonging and well-being during the school day. Their answers differ very little from those of pupils without disabilities in this respect. According to the teachers, the pupils with disabilities are not teased or troubled by the others. The mean of the values for the pupils with disabilities differs only slightly from the corresponding figure for the others, indicating that the pupils with disabilities as a group:

- experience the same level of well-being at school as do the others;
- are not more lonely;
- have closer contact with teachers and assistants than do most of the pupils without disabilities; and
- have a curriculum adapted to their individual needs

It is possible that acceptance and social initiative on the part of the pupils without disabilities have a positive influence on the well-being of those with disabilities and on their self-esteem and quality of life.

It seems that both the schools are developing into socially inclusive primary schools in accordance with the principle of an inclusive school for all.

What factors could promote good social interaction between handicapped and non-handicapped pupils ? The study indicates that the following may be particularly important:

1. Organisational factors

- systematic co-operation between ordinary teachers and special teachers;
- the head teacher's attitude towards integration;
- a well-planned timetable; and,
- teacher training.

2. Using existing "meeting points" for pupils with and without disabilities, and creating new ones

The concept of a "meeting place" is useful when describing structured social contexts.

3. Individualised education

The teachers who participated in the study consider that, if the social integration of pupils with disabilities is to succeed, the programmes of education for these pupils must be adapted to each one's individual needs. They should be linked up, however, to the National Curriculum and the curriculum for the class.

4. Consultants

The teachers at both schools think that if programmes of integration are to be initiated and maintained, it is necessary to have both internal and external advisers with special competence in teaching pupils with disabilities. Internal advisers are considered more important than external ones, which probably reflects a desire for advice at the time it is needed. Team teaching and regular evaluation of the individual programmes are also important.

The study seems to show an association between the special educational programmes for the pupils with disabilities and the social education of these pupils.

Integration of pupils with disabilities into the school environment should be the responsibility of the whole school, not of just a few teachers. It seems that greater effort is needed at organisational, teacher and pupil level if the integration is to be more successful.

This view of the school and education seems to be important for achieving a school for all kinds of pupils, which gives priority to creating good conditions for social participation and interaction, since this is a prerequisite for social integration.

New white papers

White Paper No. 29 (1994-95) has recently been adopted by the Storting (Norwegian National Assembly). It contains guidelines for extending compulsory education to ten years (called Reform '97), and for a new National Curriculum. It emphasises the principle of an all-inclusive school, where an over-riding concept is education adapted to individual needs.

The Ministry will now start to work out guidelines for preparing special programmes of individual education. These will emphasise the need for plans which also describe "meeting places", to promote social participation and integration. Individual learning programmes should also be considered in the context of the overall plan for habilitation, including after-school activities.

Several educational reforms are being implemented in Norway today. Reform '97 is at the planning stage. Reform '94, giving all young people who have completed compulsory schooling a right to upper secondary education, is already effective. Both reforms also apply to children requiring special education.

One of the Ministry's objectives in the years ahead is to makes matters of special education, and the development work in this field, a natural and visible part of all spheres of activity in the school system, also when implementing any further reforms in the education sector.

Further studies are required to identify factors related to successful implementation of the ideology of an all-inclusive school in Norway. More knowledge is needed about various curriculum adaptation models, the effects of various components of integration models, and how to balance the particular needs of the pupil on the one hand with regular classroom integration and social experience on the other.

It is hoped that the Ministry's research and development (R&D) programme, established in connection with the re-organisation of special education, will contribute in this respect. It consists of two parts. Firstly, there is a five-year national research project "Knowledge and measures in the field of special education", administered by the Norwegian Research Council. The research is action-oriented, and aims at improving the situation of the users of the special education services. The second part is a decentralised development programme for local authorities, administered by the National Education Office in each county. The programme is designed and implemented in accordance with the guidelines from the Ministry, and with the education plan for the county concerned.

Another White Paper, prepared for presentation to the Storting in autumn 1996, sums up the re-structuring of special education and indicates what should be done in the future. Very many children, adolescents and adults who need special education are also users of other public services. Widespread co-operation is required across sectors if their needs are to be met satisfactorily in the local community. It asks what the government can do, across the areas of responsibility of the different ministries, to stimulate the development of parallel and co-ordinated services for persons with special needs.

Summary

A fundamental principle of Norwegian education is an all-inclusive school, where children and young people with varying abilities and aptitudes receive a meaningful education adapted to their own individuals needs, preferably without having to leave home.

Special education in the ordinary school is dependent on assistance and advice from experts, represented by the educational-psychological service, and more recently the national centres for special education (established in each county by transforming the special schools in to resource centres).

Integration of handicapped pupils in the school and the classroom requires not only individualised education programmes but also opportunities for social participation; the systematic development of "meeting places". A case study shows that non-handicapped pupils accept handicapped pupils and take a social initiative towards them at school, but not so much after school hours. This acceptance by fellow pupils has a positive affect on the handicapped pupils' well-being and self-esteem (Nordahl and Overland, 1993).

The case study shows that various factors are important for good social interaction between handicapped and non-handicapped pupils: organisational factors, "meeting places", individualised education programmes, and internal and external consultants.

Several reforms are being implemented in the Norwegian school system. Reform '94, giving all pupils who have completed compulsory schooling a right to upper secondary education has already been put into effect. Reform '97, which extends compulsory education to ten years (as against nine at present) is at the planning stage. It is emphasised that both these reforms also apply to students with special needs.

A research and development programme has been started to obtain the knowledge needed to provide meaningful and individually adapted education for students with special needs, and integrate them effectively into the ordinary school. The programme consists of two parts, a national research programme and a development programme in the counties.

In the future, it will be an objective to make matters of special education, and the associated development work, a natural and visible part of all spheres of activity in the school system.

Part IV

SUPPORT

CHAPTER 16

PARENTAL, ADVISORY AND ADMINISTRATIVE SUPPORT IN OECD COUNTRIES

by

Don Labon

Introduction

Integration can be considered from various perspectives. One may choose to focus on units of differing size: child, teacher, class, school, district, region, nation. Which unit is the most influential? A clear feature of the reports contributing to the OECD project is the recognition of the importance of the ordinary school as a unit.

The school as a whole can be a central force in the implementation of any integration programme. If the staff of the school are united in their resolve to make integration work, and if they have the skills and the material resources needed, then they are in a powerful position to overcome the inevitable difficulties arising. Nevertheless, there must be times when even the most courageous of head-teachers feel at the mercy of forces outside the school, and must wonder about the extent to which these forces are benign or hostile. They may even come to the following view, as expressed in Giraudoux's *Electra:*

> "I believe in the gods. But I don't believe that they are great brooding presences watching over us; I believe that they are completely absent-minded."

This paper considers external forces, brooding or otherwise, of three different kinds: *parental, advisory,* and *administrative*. Firstly, mainly on the basis of the country reports provided for the OECD project, it looks at the *contributions* these three groups have made to integration in different countries. Secondly, on the basis of case studies submitted, it selects a few telling *examples*. Finally, drawing on both sets of documentation, it outlines what appear to be features of *good practice* with respect to each group.

Parental contributions

Parents may contribute individually, on behalf of their own children, or collectively, on behalf of children with disabilities more generally. Active members of parental organisations are not typical of parents more generally; they tend to be of higher than average socio-economic status. When they act as representatives, on the governing bodies of schools for example, the fact that they are present does not necessarily mean that they are influential or even that they participate to any great extent.

In many countries parents have played an active role in the development of special education. In doing so they have often been members of national organisations concerned with disabilities.

Sometimes -- the German "Parents Against Separation" group has been presented as an example -- these organisations also have a significant number of members who are parents only of children without disabilities.

Parents in many countries, including Canada, Denmark, Norway, Spain, Sweden, the United Kingdom and the United States, have been influential over many years in their countries' moves towards integration. Reports from Australia, Belgium, Greece, Iceland and the Netherlands also testify to the fact that parents continue to be very active as advocates. In some instances they have pressed ordinary schools to implement existing legislation in providing integrative programmes, for example in physical education, the performing arts, social development and community involvement.

Not all parents favour integration. The reports from Denmark, Ireland, the Netherlands and Norway, for example, referred to some parents as preferring segregated settings. They tended to be parents of children with severe learning disabilities, who in fact constitute only a small proportion of children with special needs. Some parents of deaf children, too, expressed reservations.

Parents are regularly involved in assessment. In some countries their involvement is prescribed in legislation. In the United States, for example, children with special needs are entitled to multi-disciplinary assessment, an individualised education plan and placement in the most integrated setting thought suitable, and parents must be consulted regarding the placement. The position is similar in several other OECD countries, including Belgium, Denmark, France and the United Kingdom.

Despite some countries' firm commitment to partnership with parents, there is much evidence to indicate that this is not always carried through into everyday practice. One reported difficulty was that laws were observed in such a way as to provide a symbolic reassurance of procedural fairness without enabling parents to affect the outcome of assessments. Another was professionals' use of technical jargon incomprehensible to lay people. Another was providing opportunity for parents to react to professionals' decisions but not to participate in the decision-making process.

Parental involvement in the day-to-day provision of schools has been found to take various forms: marginal, consultative, participative and managerial.

- Marginal involvement is usually formalised and sometimes ritualistic, featuring in ceremonial activities such as open days, in which parents tend to be members of an audience.

- Consultative involvement is likely to be more frequent, more informal and more varied. Parents not only receive information and advice but also provide it.

- Participative involvement is also likely to be extensive and informal, though it may well occur within a structured framework. Parents may, for example, help teachers in the classroom.

- Managerial involvement requires the services of only a small proportion of parents, and usually consists of serving on the school's governing body. It is an important aspect of the running of schools and in some OECD countries is a legal requirement.

Sometimes parents are involved in designing their own teaching programmes. The most extensive example is that of the Portage system, first developed in the United States in the early 1970s for use with pre-school children and subsequently adapted to meet the needs of many OECD countries. In a typical session, parent and trained home visitor together engage the child in activities, assess the child's skills and set short-term teaching targets. The visitor may demonstrate teaching methods. The parent teaches the child and records progress on activity charts. Subsequent visits help the parent to review progress and decide on further activities. In recent years the system has been extended for use in schools.

Contributions of advisers

Whereas parents are usually easily identified as such, this is not necessarily the case with advisers. In special education, the nature of the support they provide varies considerably from one country to another and support service staff with similar job titles in different countries may fulfil different roles. In many countries the range of support services is highly complex, with significant regional variation and with different groups of professionals working for different organisations that may be largely independent of one another.

Many of the people involved are teachers with specialist qualifications; some are qualified as psychologists. People contributing to multi-disciplinary work may include speech therapists, doctors and social workers. Some advisory services, particularly those involving in-service training, are provided by staff of universities and colleges.

One of the functions of support service staff is to advise on allocation of children to one or other form of special education. If the children are placed in ordinary schools, then in most OECD countries allocation is informal and need not involve these external services. In the New Brunswick region of Canada, for example, the ordinary school's managing body can allocate resources informally without reference to any outside group and parents can be involved in choosing from a range of in-school services. Similar informalities exist in Australia, Norway and to some extent in Greece. In Iceland, short-term help can be provided informally but long-term support is conditional on recommendations arising from formal assessment procedures.

In some countries the provision of extra teaching help or equipment to support special education even in ordinary classes can be conditional on formal multi-disciplinary assessment and on decisions at regional or even national level. The English "statement" system and the Italian "certificate" arrangements provide examples of these degrees of formality and centralisation.

The employment of peripatetic teachers to provide specialist advice and in-class support across a range of ordinary schools is a regular feature of special education in many countries, including Austria, Belgium, Finland, Germany, Ireland, the Netherlands, Norway, Spain and the United Kingdom. It tends to occur in rural areas with small scattered schools, and here may sometimes be a response to the problems of wide dispersal of children with special needs rather than a conscious attempt to support full integration. It can also be found in some urban areas, however, where it is clearly integrationist in intent and where it also enables one person's special education expertise to influence several schools.

Support services are sometimes provided by staff of special schools. As the role of the special school is the topic of the third theme of the conference, I propose to do no more than mention it here. Suffice it to say that organised co-operation of this kind exists in many countries, including Austria, France, Germany, Greece, Iceland, the Netherlands and the United Kingdom.

Across OECD countries, support services are often organised on a regional basis. Many countries have child guidance and counselling services, though their functions vary from one country to another. For example, In Germany their work includes helping families and teachers tackle learning difficulties and solve problems concerning careers, whereas in Greece the school counsellor appointed to each district also offers advice on the curriculum and on teaching methods more generally.

The work of district or regional special education advisers and inspectors, as seen in the United Kingdom for example, includes providing professional advice, monitoring provision and organising in-service training. Some of this work overlaps with that of educational psychologists, who assess children's learning difficulties, offer counselling and contribute to placement decisions. Psychological services in Finland, France, Iceland, Italy, Norway and Switzerland follow a similar pattern. Not all regional support to schools is organised on the basis of educational services; in Ireland, for example, health services are very active in this field.

The job of teaching children with special needs in ordinary classes is complex, and the teachers concerned are continually facing new challenges. Because of this, virtually all teachers need to have access to advice about special education both before and after they qualify as teachers. At both stages, some of this support is provided by staff of teacher training establishments.

In initial teacher training, establishments in only some of the OECD countries include special educational needs issues for all students as yet, but the position is improving. Such facilities already exist in Canada, France, Italy, Norway, and the United Kingdom. They are a requirement across most of the United States. There are some such opportunities in Iceland and in Spain, and there are moves in this direction in Belgium, Germany, Greece and Switzerland.

Specialist courses, leading to advanced diplomas or higher degrees, designed for teachers wishing to specialise in special education, exist across OECD countries. Their availability to teachers, however, varies considerably. As countries implement their integration policies, these courses provide important training routes for teachers undertaking special education support work in ordinary schools as well as for those wishing to work in special schools. The general trend is for this training to be undertaken after basic initial training and after a period of work in ordinary schools. From the point of view of integration, this trend is to be welcomed.

Teacher training establishments also run a variety of short courses, which do not necessarily lead to advanced qualifications. Some are designed to influence attitudes. Some are designed to familiarise class teachers in ordinary schools with special needs issues. Some provide direct training in teaching methods that enable children with special needs to progress in integrated settings. Staff of teacher training establishments are by no means alone in this. Other support staff, both within and outside schools, provide such training.

Effective short-term development work of this kind, suitable for all school staff, is essential if integration programmes are to succeed. Among the various contributions to the second phase of the project, those from Australia were exceptionally valuable from this point of view. They included detailed descriptions and evaluations of a variety of training packages, covering a broad range of topics and designed for use by support staff in many different settings.

Some special education support services operate at national level. In the Netherlands, for example, there are national as well as regional educational advisory centres. Whereas the regional services support elementary and some special schools, the three national advisory centres are mainly concerned with secondary school counselling and with implementing educational innovation across the system. In Norway, some of the special schools are being transformed into national resource centres which will provide information and offer counselling. In Spain, a national resource centre for special education provides information, offers teacher training and conducts research. In Japan, the national institute for special education carries similar functions, in association with an adjacent special school and 27 regional centres. In Finland the national centre undertakes curriculum development.

Contributions of administrators

Quite apart from the question as to whether the allocation of funds for children with special needs is sufficient, there is the question as to whether the money available is allocated in such a way as to encourage integration. The following focuses on the second of these questions.

Counting the cost is fraught with difficulty. None of the country reports has been able to present precise costing of special education in different settings. Nevertheless, as far as we can tell, and in general terms, costing favours integration. For the vast majority of children with special needs, education in integrated settings does not appear to be inordinately costly and in any case it is less expensive than their placement in special schools.

Member countries of the OECD differ considerably in their methods of allocating funds for special education. In the Netherlands, for example, ordinary and special education come under separate systems, whereas in the New Brunswick region of Canada and in Norway they come under one. In Finland, where funding is partly at national level, the government pays 70 per cent of education costs for most children but 86 per cent for some children with severe disabilities.

In Iceland, special schools are funded entirely at national level but ordinary schools at district level. In the New Brunswick region of Canada, funding for ordinary schools is based on a block formula that assumes a given percentage of children with special needs, but there are exceptions under certain circumstances. Ordinary schools in the United Kingdom, similarly, receive core funding for children with special needs generally but also receive additional funding for individuals with particular disabilities.

Overall experience of the effects of these different funding systems indicates that factors conducive to integration include the financing of ordinary school and special school education under one umbrella, realistic allowances being made to ordinary schools for the extra costs of educating children with special needs generally, and further specific allowances being made for the small minority of children whose special needs carry particular resource implications. Within an overall policy fostering integration, it would seem reasonable to tip the balance of resourcing slightly in favour of special education within ordinary classes, for example by providing bonuses to reward good progress.

Examples of parental involvement

While some parents have been instrumental in initiating integration programmes and acting as advocates for their children with disabilities, they are atypical, as the following extract from a report of the work of an Icelandic school indicates.

"(...) parents interviewed seem to view the school as the 'expert' in their child's education and are reluctant to ask questions, interfere, complain, or make suggestions, even when they do not agree with the school. Therefore, parents rarely confront the school openly and the messages to the school are often subtle and informal. This reluctance on behalf of parents is not because they find the school unapproachable; on the contrary, all of the parents emphasise that they find the school personnel, both administrators and teachers, accessible and easy to talk to".

In this same school, however, some of the parents of children with special needs were rather more proactive, as can be seen from the following extract.

"The parents of students with special needs, who were interviewed, were overwhelmingly pleased with how their school had responded to their children's educational needs. Many of them, however, pointed out that they -- not the school -- had been the ones who discovered the child's problem. They had also been the ones who pressured the school to respond to the child's needs. The parents emphasised the importance of advocating on behalf of their children. They agreed that if parents do not advocate for their children they run the risk of not receiving proper educational services."

The following extract, from a United States contribution, provides some indication of the influence that the range of parental and broader community involvement can have on a school.

"The school organises foster grandparent, parent volunteer, and peer tutoring programs which are available to all students. Students with moderate or severe disabilities have a big brother/sister program available on a limited basis, particularly for students labelled severely emotionally disturbed. Parent support groups offer some assistance to parents of students with moderate and severe disabilities. Some local business and community organisations have donated equipment for students with severe disabilities. Local religious and athletic organisations offer community recreation programs, especially for older students who need career or vocational experiences. The local mental health agency is involved with a few students with moderate and severe disabilities.

Some businesses and business organisations provide opportunities for students with disabilities who are in financial need. In addition, other organisations often provide opportunities for students with moderate and severe disabilities to attend summer camps or local recreation camps, and will under certain conditions purchase or loan to families necessary equipment."

Examples of the work of advisers

Most of the case study reports acknowledged the existence of external support services. In general, they gave the impression that support services were offered by many people, with varying kinds and levels of expertise, but that they often had only marginal influence on the schools. Multidisciplinary services seemed to be concerned largely with diagnosis and advice on children's educational placement rather than with help with teaching methods. There were some references, however, to peripatetic teachers and to special education advisers as providing this kind of help. Also, as the following extract from a case study report of a school in the United Kingdom shows, some local education authorities (LEAs) vigorously promoted in-service education and training (INSET) aimed at curriculum development.

"There was a considerable amount of activity in the LEA as regards INSET on matters relating to provision for pupils with special educational needs. There were various curriculum guidelines and teachers were working across discrete special needs areas. There was also a "Special educational needs and the National Curriculum" forum organised by the special needs inspector and there were meetings for every special school teacher, service staff and special needs co-ordinators. There had been a lot of work on the whole curriculum."

A striking example of a successful special education support service emerged from the Canadian case study. This showed the work of a district's student services team to be highly valued in schools, primarily because it concentrated on helping teachers develop their own skills rather than focusing on assessment and placement of individual children.

"(...) the School District Number 12 student services team supports the schools in a variety of ways such as by providing professional development training, bi-weekly meetings for the methods and resource teachers, and indirect and direct interventions, and by problem-solving. School staff and parents indicated that district office staff have been a strong support team and their leadership has influenced the development and success of integration in the schools. Many school staff felt that integration would not have happened without the leadership, commitment and support from the School District Number 12 student services team".

Another example of a successful external support service came from the Netherlands, where the networking of 28 co-operating elementary schools was co-ordinated by the region's education advice centre (the OAB).

"Teachers were uniformly positive about it, finding in it a source of mutual support, an opportunity for sharing experiences and problems, and a major arena for professional development. The network seems to have a non-competitive ethos, with staff building on each other's strengths and learning a great deal from each other (...).

The network is not confined to special education. Indeed it seems to operate across a wide range of the functions of the schools -- curriculum policy, staff deployment and resourcing, indicating that a wider process of innovation is taking place in these schools. Thus, the school co-operation which permits the degree of integration that is taking place is not defined in terms of pupils with learning difficulties; to that extent the integration initiative is a normal part of the life of the schools (...).

The OAB appears to play a critical role. Without its animating influence it is unlikely that the school networking or the integration initiative would have developed."

It is worth noting that in each of these three examples the focus was on the work of the school as a whole, and that the people for whom the support was being provided were those likely to be particularly influential promoters of integration within their own schools.

Administrative support

Effective administrative support can be exemplified by reference to the context within which the advisory staff referred to in the Canadian case study worked. The district's senior administrative staff had for many years vigorously promoted integration, had consulted extensively before implementing integration initiatives, had encouraged progressive replacement of ordinary schools' special classes by resource rooms and in-class support, had closed the district's special schools, had distributed funds to the ordinary schools in accordance with the learning needs of the children on roll, had financed ongoing training at district level for key teachers, and had supported further dissemination of this training within the schools themselves.

Good practice

The project's country reports and case study reports yielded a wealth of information useful to the planning, initiation, implementation and evaluation of integration programmes at all levels, ranging from the national to the individual. The following features of good practice, with regard to sources of support external to the schools themselves, are likely to appear as integration programmes become established.

Good practice in parental and community involvement

- At all stages of national developments in integration, representatives of parent organisations are involved on a consultative basis.

- As district and within-school integration programmes are developed, parents of children with special needs, along with representatives of the communities more generally, are consulted from the outset of each stage and are invited to participate.

- When parents of children with special educational needs seek to initiate or further develop integration programmes, their views are taken as seriously by decision-makers as are those of professionals.

- Parents are treated as partners in assessment, decision-making and review when their children are being considered by staff of schools and external support services with a view to special educational provision.

- Parents of children with special educational needs are represented on the governing bodies of schools.

- Where appropriate, parents and other members of the community are encouraged to be present in classrooms and to share in the work of the schools.

- Parents of children with special needs, particularly parents of pre-school children, are helped by professionals to develop the skills needed to teach their own children.

- Parents are helped by school and external support service staff to develop advocacy skills, where needed, including those of negotiation.

Good practice among advisory services

- Staff of external support services apply and develop their advisory and in-service training skills, particularly in relation to within-school support staff, rather than focusing largely on assessment and placement.

- Staff of support services negotiate specific and finite arrangements, including learning targets, for the support they are to provide.

- Staff of support services, in consultation with school staff and parents, plan and monitor the transition of students with special needs from schools to suitable post-school experience.

- Staff of external support services, outreach staff of special schools, and staff of teacher training establishments confer to ensure that their services are complementary and together meet local needs.

- Initial teacher training courses ensure that all trainees gain awareness of special needs, some knowledge of disabilities and some skills in teaching children of varying abilities in normal classes.

- Initial teacher training courses provide options enabling trainees with particular interests and aptitudes in special education to develop further knowledge and skills.

- Teacher training establishments meet the needs for training to higher degree level in all major aspects of special education, including training to apply the expertise gained in fulfilling researching, innovating, inspectorial, administrative, managerial, advisory and teacher training roles.

Good practice in administration

- Government, regional and district education policies state that wherever practicable children with special educational needs should be educated in ordinary classes in ordinary schools.

- Policy makers at all levels regularly reaffirm their commitment to integration and take opportunities, for example by publicising successful examples, to promote and sustain positive attitudes, among children, among teachers and among other adults in the community, towards those with special needs.

- Government, regional and district education authorities monitor, evaluate and actively review the implementation of their integration policies.

- Regional and district education authorities monitor provision of in-service training arrangements in special education, to ensure that the needs of all their schools are met effectively.

- District education authorities ensure that the progress of children with significant disabilities is monitored and that their provision is reviewed periodically.

- Where formal assessment of children's special needs is undertaken, this involves consultation with parents and draws on appropriate specialisms but does not cause inordinate delay in securing appropriate provision.

- District education authorities ensure that children with special needs have access to educational opportunities in integrated settings well before they reach statutory school age.

- At national level, distribution of educational resources does not encourage regional and district authorities to place children with special needs in special schools rather than in ordinary schools.

- The distribution of resources to schools takes realistic account of the differences in expenditure required to provide appropriate education for children of differing abilities, and in doing so builds in some incentives for teachers in ordinary schools to provide for children with special needs in ordinary classes.

- Resourcing of integration programmes allows for their being relatively costly at initiation and during the earlier stages of their implementation, and takes realistic account of the costs of continued monitoring once they are established. Evaluation is built into the programmes from the start.

CHAPTER 17

THE INFLUENCE OF RELATED SERVICES ON EDUCATIONAL INTEGRATION IN THE UNITED STATES

by

Martha Coutinho and Alan C. Repp

Through a broad-based national commitment and the provision of comprehensive services and programs, the United States fosters the preparedness of individuals with disabilities to assume productive adult lives. The national mandate to provide a free appropriate public education (FAPE) to children and youth with disabilities is a primary objective. The Individuals with Disabilities Education Act (IDEA: Public law 102-229), first passed as Public Law 94-142 in 1975, embodies the national commitment to provide opportunities that will contribute to the educational progress of children with disabilities. As provided in IDEA, children with disabilities represent those children who because of their disability need special education and related services. Special education represents the delivery of "specially designed instruction", related services (which may be described as external services), and other supports, when necessary, that are designed to meet the unique needs of a student with disabilities.

Implementing major reforms and confronting significant fiscal restraints and cutbacks, schools increasingly seek to improve the outcomes and to provide for the education of children with disabilities with their non-disabled peers. Through national initiatives (*e.g.*, school choice and outcome-based educational approaches) and wide-scale innovation, educators in the United States are implementing programs that are intended to address six National Education Goals for all students. The urgency for doing so has increased, as evidence accumulates that outcomes for children and youth with disabilities are poor, and that preparedness for adult life and the quality of life achieved do not meet national intent or expectations (Wagner *et al.*, 1991). With increasing momentum, but not without controversy and complexity, American schools are expanding the capacity of systems to meet the needs of students with disabilities.

IDEA also provides that children with disabilities be educated, to the maximum extent appropriate, with children who are not disabled. Known as the "Least Restrictive Environment" requirement, this principle affirms the importance and supports the integration of students with disabilities. Special education is not a place, but represents instruction, related services, and supports based on individual student need and not on administrative convenience. Many of the implications for the provision of integrated educational opportunities have been presented elsewhere (Sloan, Alberg *et al.*, 1992).

The difficulties and complexities associated with the provision of an integrated or inclusive education have led to the identification of many issues and barriers related to implementation as well. For example, the National Education Association (NEA, 1992) supports the education of students with disabilities in the least restrictive environment, but notes many requisites (fiscal, personnel, administrative, etc.) that are required to implement fully the least restrictive environment mandate. Issues related to the design of curricula, assessment, and the impact of school restructuring efforts have been presented in a descriptive case study prepared for the OECD (Sloan, Alberg *et al.,* 1992).

Recent years, have witnessed significant growth in the knowledge base that exists to support the successful integration of children with disabilities. These approaches draw upon best practice in regular and special education and from systems change. Despite increasing commitment and efforts to provide for the integration of students with disabilities, significant national progress must still be made. Based upon data reported annually by the States across all disabilities and for the 1989-1990 school year, 7 per cent of all student with disabilities received their education in separate facilities. Within general education settings, over 60 per cent of all children with disabilities received educational services *outside* of the regular class. Stated differently, slightly less than one-third of all children with disabilities are educated within regular classes.

This placement pattern has been remarkably stable over the last several years. For students with high incidence disabilities (learning disabilities, speech or language impairments, mental retardation, and serious emotional disturbance), the percentage change in placement in regular class/resource room combined from 1985-86 to 1989-90 is slightly negative -- meaning fewer children were placed in regular class/resource room arrangements. For all disabilities combined, there has been a 0.2 per cent increase over the same 14-year time period (United States Department of Education, 1992).

Current policy initiatives continue to support the integration of students with disabilities and to promote better outcomes for children and youth with disabilities. In 1986, former Assistant Secretary Will encouraged innovative, integrated models of service delivery and described "a shared responsibility" between regular and special education. More recently, the US Office of Special Education Programs established as a strategic target an effort to secure and expand access and inclusion for children with disabilities. Tom Hehir, current Director of the US Office of Special Education Programs, recently described characteristics of "Restructured Inclusive Schools" for all children (Hehir, 1993). Finally, The National Association of State Boards of Education (NASBE) recently completed a two-year study of special education. In their report, "Winners All", they recommended, particularly in light of the equation-reform movement, the "creation of an inclusive system that strives to produce better outcomes for all students" (NASBE, 1992).

Earlier, we noted that special education was defined as specially designed instruction and related services. As an external service, related services significantly influence efforts to integrate children with disabilities. As provided in IDEA, related services represent:

"transportation, and such developmental, corrective, and other supportive services (including speech pathology and audiology, psychological services, physical and occupational therapy, recreation, including therapeutic recreation and social work services and medical and counselling services, including rehabilitation counselling, except that such medical services shall be of diagnostic and evaluation purposes only) *as may be required to assist a child with a disability to benefit from special education*, and includes the early identification and assessment of disabling conditions in children".

Therefore, related services must be provided, but may be provided *only* when necessary to assist a child with disabilities to benefit from special education. A significant exception to this requirement is provided in IDEA for infants and toddlers (birth through two years of age). For these children, related services (such as physical therapy, occupational therapy, and speech pathology services) are defined directly as early intervention services.

A report by The National Council on Disability ("The Education of Students with Disabilities: Where Do We Stand?") presented well over two dozen findings regarding the relationship between special education and related services. In many respects, this report represented a call for change on the part of providers of related services and for the way related services are to be provided and understood within schools (Huffman, 1991). In the last several years there has been increasing attention focused upon the need for approaches and models of service delivery that emphasise the provision of related services within regular education settings (*e.g.*, Anderson and Nelson, 1988; Norris and Hoffman, 1990; O'Brien and O'Leary, 1988). Today, "related services professionals are often employed directly by school systems and provide therapeutic intervention and consultation in classrooms or related settings" (Ottenbacher, 1991, p. 10).

The influence of related services upon the integration of students with disabilities is far reaching (Coutinho, 1991). For example, IDEA also provides for a multidisciplinary evaluation to determine the need for special education and related services. Related service providers must work as members of a team that includes educators, parents, and other specialists to determine if a child is eligible for services, what shall be provided, and in what settings services will be provided. With the passage of a definition of early intervention services that includes related services for infants and toddlers with disabilities (as described above), related service providers now participate as multidisciplinary team members in the development of individualised family service plans for infants and toddlers. These plans must state the natural environments in which early intervention services shall appropriately be provided, to the maximum extent appropriate, in natural environments, including the home and community settings in which children without disabilities participate.

While increasing the offering of related services in educational settings, providers have developed additional skills focused upon program and service planning that has direct application to educational goals, objectives, and settings (Campbell, McInerney and Cooper, 1984; Mullins, 1981; Ottenbacher, 1991). Training programs and ongoing professional development opportunities have been offered to assist related services personnel in the transition from functioning in traditional medically-oriented environments to educational settings (Gilfoyle and Hays, 1979; Ottenbacher, 1991). Licensure and certification issues and problems have emerged as States seek to define what constitutes "qualified" in educational settings when provided by teachers and related service providers.

Progressively, the effects of related services upon the integration of students with disabilities is being influenced by an evolution in the nature of philosophical approaches offered to link, align, and integrate those services provided by educators and related service providers. This process has been complicated and uneven, but philosophical perspectives and issues regarding *a)* models of interactions and *b)* service delivery that must be consistent with IDEA and mutually reinforcing for the successful integration of students with disabilities to occur. McCormick and Lee (1979) described the relationship between educators and related services providers as a mandated partnership, stating that IDEA:

"focused national attention on the importance of working partnerships and teamwork to the delivery of optimally effective services to handicapped children. In addition to competencies in

125

evaluation, instructional planning, therapy, and consultation, professionals must resolve past differences (real or imagined) and demonstrate co-operation, collaboration and communication" (p. 580).

Therefore, the influence of related services upon the integration of students with disabilities, in turn, is greatly affected by the disciplinary and philosophical perspectives of educators versus those of related service personnel with respect to models of interaction and service provision.

With respect to models of interaction, recent years have seen tremendous growth in the implementation of *team* approaches to service delivery. Prior to the passage of IDEA and in traditional arrangements, provision of related services has reflected a uni-disciplinary orientation. Working in separate, and primarily non-educational settings, related service providers, each representing a separate discipline (*e.g.*, physical therapy, speech therapy, etc.), conducted independent evaluations, formulated separate treatment goals, and implemented plans independently. Consumers, parents, and educators were rarely involved.

Multidisciplinary team approaches have extended upon the uni-disciplinary approach to include sharing among team members the results of evaluations, who represent various disciplines and kinds of related service. Interventions, however, are typically implemented directly by related service providers in settings that are traditional for that discipline and related service. Inter-disciplinary team approaches take collaboration one step further -- goals and objectives for intervention and treatment are shared by all members of the team; and, where possible, they are co-ordinated.

The integration of children with disabilities has been significantly influenced by the provision of related services that reflect a trans-disciplinary team approach. This model has been described as well-suited to the provision of integrated services in complex educational environments (Giangreco, 1990; Rainforth and York, 1987; Sparling, 1980; York, Rainforth and Giangreco, 1990). The trans-disciplinary approach is based on the belief that services, philosophies, and personnel must be integrated and must include parents as professional partners. Quoting Ottenbacher (1991, pp. 22-23), Berndt and Falconer (1991) suggested that trans-disciplinary team approaches have the following characteristics:

- programming is a joint effort by all team members;
- the members of the team share their expertise and skills with each other;
- assessment is related to the student's functional abilities in specific environments rather than being referenced to a specific discipline performing the evaluation; and,
- responsibility for achieving program objectives is shared through a "role release" process.

"Team members are encouraged to "release" some of their skills to others, so that intervention is continuous and not bound to a single discipline" (Berndt and Falconer, 1991). Assessment, goals, and intervention focus on the student, not on respective disciplines, as professionals share roles and expertise. In this model, parents represent an external service similar to the related services. As described by Dunn and Campbell (1991), generally "one person implements the program, becoming the child's primary service provider or program facilitator" (p. 127). As schools increasingly integrate students with disabilities, that role is often assumed by the teacher.

The extent of integration for a child with disabilities may also be affected by the methods by which the related services are provided. Dunn (1988) describes three approaches: direct service, monitoring, and consultation. Direct service is the traditional model in which the related service provider works directly with one or a very small number of students, and is personally responsible for the intervention. The educational relevance of the goals of therapy and the intervention must be established. In the monitoring model of service provision, the related service provider will function directly to identify student needs and to plan appropriate intervention; however, the related service personnel then train and assist others in implementing the intervention. In consultation, related service providers depart from traditional roles. The specialised knowledge of the related service provider is used to:

"facilitate the workings of the educational system. Consultation in the educational environment is oriented toward the needs of *a)* the student, *b)* professionals, or *c)* the system; in practice, these forms often occur together. Case consultation addresses the student's needs, focusing on developing the most effective educational environment for a specific student. Colleague consultation addresses the needs of other professional to improve their skills and knowledge. System consultation improves the effectiveness of the agency or district by addressing the needs of generic groups within the system" (Dunn, 1988, p. 720).

In recent years, increasing numbers of related services personnel are being trained to function in the consultation and monitoring roles to respond to the increasing integration and need for a greater breadth of services in educational settings (Royeen and Coutinho, 1992). The consultative approach may be expected to increase further with the continuing emphasis upon trans-disciplinary teams (Ottenbacher, 1991).

Parents may also be described as an external factor that significantly affects the integration of children with disabilities. IDEA sets forth several protections and requirements for parental participation. Parents retain numerous rights, remedies, and opportunities that are intended to ensure their full consent and involvement in decisions affecting eligibility, assessment, and the services and settings in which instruction and related services are provided. With respect to early intervention services, parental involvement is particularly critical.

In summary, the provision of related services has many implications and raises many issues that influence the integration of children and youth with disabilities. These include:

- professional training, development, and support for educators, parents and related service providers;
- assignment of accountability for the goals and outcomes of services;
- implementation of team-based models of interaction within schools engaged in educational reform and restructuring;
- assessment of relative costs and benefits associated with various models of service provision (*e.g.*, direct, consultative or monitoring); and,
- the role of parents as an external service and a participant in the planning, implementation, and/or receipt of services.

In conclusion, a national commitment and ongoing effort is underway in the United States to foster the preparedness of individuals with disabilities to assume productive adult lives. As a part of the mandate to provide a free appropriate public education to children and youth with disabilities, professionals, parents and educators are increasing efforts to integrate children with disabilities successfully and to provide special education and related services in general education settings. How related services are defined and provided significantly influences the integration of children with disabilities. Traditional models of interaction and service delivery are being supplemented or replaced on an increasing basis by more interactive approaches (*e.g.*, the trans-disciplinary model, in which the focus is on the student, not on respective disciplines). Professionals share roles and expertise, and parents represent an external service similar to other related services. In these approaches, teachers assume significant and often primary responsibility for facilitating or providing the program. The specialised and professional expertise of related service providers is shared with educators on a systematic, collaborative and interactive basis.

As the models for service provision and interaction evolve, several issues and implications for the successful integration of children with disabilities may be identified, including how best to support the need for additional training and support for professionals, the assignment of accountability for the goals and outcomes of services, the interface between the provision of specially-designed instruction and related services and other initiatives at the school building level (*i.e.*, reform and restructuring), and the relative costs, benefits, and outcomes associated with various models of provision of related services.

CHAPTER 18

PARENTAL, STATUTORY AND VOLUNTARY SUPPORT SERVICES IN BELGIUM

by

Jean-Jacques Detraux

Introduction

Integration has to be regarded as a process involving various actors. Those persons have to attempt to experience an authentic partnership in such a way that the whole process benefits the person with a disability. School integration is only a part of this process. Therefore it is important to adopt a developmental perspective and divide the process into successive steps, each of them having specific modalities according to the age of the person with disabilities, the content of short and long term goals and available resources in the environment.

This paper focuses on the importance of the role of parents as "negotiators" of a project for their children, on the necessity to develop networks and, in particular at a school level, on the necessity to develop functional links between regular and special services. Finally, the paper promotes a constructive dialogue between the formal system (granted services) and the informal services (non-profit voluntary associations).

Role of parents

Parents are more and more considered as indispensable partners. However, in many cases, behind this evidence, an ambivalent position does exist. In practice, our educational systems refer continuously to a segregative rather than a mainstreamed ideology, and confuse children's needs with their disabilities. The trend to make pseudo-scientific categories and to fund schools according to a certain number of so-labelled children is still alive in different countries. Schools in general and special schools in particular continue to act as "supermarkets", attempting to retain their "clients" for as long a period as possible.

The involvement of parents in the development and the conduct of the educational plan are not yet really implemented in our tradition. Moreover, the parents feel themselves to be deprived of their own competencies in educating their children.

Today more and more parents, younger and better informed, having experienced the positive contribution of early intervention services, approach the school system with a clear will to negotiate the best solutions for their children with disabilities. In some cases, they are taking into consideration alternatives to the special school and want to attempt a dialogue with staff of the ordinary school. The dynamic generated by this attempt is very interesting. In fact, parents are actively requested to seek a service, not for its assumed value (a special school is indeed regarded by the majority of professionals as having the necessary adequate resources for the child with disabilities), but for its capacity to create, innovate and meet others' human values.

Furthermore, a "mediator" will be involved, who will help parents to achieve their goals but will also remind the staff of the ordinary school (as well as the parents of children without disabilities) that the aim is to allow the child with disabilities to progress in learning situations and not simply to welcome the child as an act of generosity.

Parents are involved in every step of the process of integration. They gain maturity by this involvement and become progressively conscious both of the capacities and the limits of the child. In order to encourage parents to experience such a dynamic process, it is important to develop associations which put parents and professionals together, thus giving them opportunities to learn how to become real partners.

Development of networks

The common distinction between special school and ordinary school systems has to be surmounted. In fact, the critical question is how to promote at a local level the creation of networks grouping various services, notably those concerned with education, health and welfare. The great amount of energy sometimes spent on demonstrating the superiority of one system over the other can act to take attention away from the fundamental question: how to mobilise all available resources in order to enhance learning in every child. An additional question is how to prevent the development of learning difficulties.

We also have to think about the development of interactions between children with and without learning disabilities in contexts other than the classroom. In fact, children between 6 and 15 years, spend more than 80 per cent of their waking time in situations that are not strictly academic. Therefore we can promote contacts between children with and without disabilities in a great variety of life-situations, helping them to achieve social as well as educational goals.

The development of such practices, based on personal encounters at a local level, with flexible modalities in functioning and with a large autonomy, with real capacities to assume responsibility for it, seems to be the right way. The initiatives to be developed must occur in the social context itself, and we have to accept in advance all the risks which are inherent to such situations in which we are facing differences. We have also to be attentive to the mechanisms allowing a greater confidence between partners as well as a progressive modification of the negative perceptions about the handicap.

Formal versus informal systems

The development of a number of non-profit or voluntary associations, which have taken initiatives to promote integration, must be taken into consideration. Some administrative authorities do not believe in the capacity of such organisations to assume a long term plan because they have insufficient resources. However, the impossibility of being able to consider long term goals and the relative insecurity that objectively exists will very often represent an opportunity for innovation thus avoiding the well-known process of ossification.

School systems are increasingly interacting with non-profit associations that offer many opportunities to organise activities in which children with disabilities and children without disabilities can participate together. A critical issue regarding this is the necessary role of a mediator to create and develop such initiatives. When the intervention of the mediator ceases, the activities are generally not continued.

Consequently we have to be attentive to the relationship between formal and non-formal structures in order to evaluate how outside-school resources can contribute to the development of the process of integration on a long-term basis.

CHAPTER 19

SCHOOL ORGANISATIONAL STRUCTURES SUPPORTING INCLUSION IN SPAIN

by

Gerardo Echeita

Introduction

The objective of this paper is to present an analysis of factors conducive to the provision of support systems that are effective in integrating pupils with special needs within the Spanish education system. Firstly, general characteristics of special education support systems in Spain are described. Secondly, those most likely to facilitate inclusive education are identified.

Spanish interest in the OECD project (OECD, 1995) has focused on the support systems, because both the Ministry of Education and the education authorities in the Autonomous Communities have made a big effort to implement those services in order to facilitate the integration of pupils with special educational needs in the ordinary schools. The analysis made in the context of this project can contribute to a better comprehension of how they operate and to improve their functioning in the future.

General characteristics of special education support systems

In Spain, in the area in which the Ministry of Education has full responsibility, but also in some autonomous communities, such as the Basque Country, traditionally the support systems have been organised in one of two ways:

- either with support teachers working from within their own mainstream schools;

- or with multiprofessional teams (including specialists in education, psychologists, social workers, speech therapists, and perhaps doctors) working from outside the schools.

In the first case, the number of support teachers in each mainstreaming school depends on the number of school units, the school population, and the kinds and numbers of pupils with special needs. The average is three teachers but, in quite a significant number of schools, the within-school support systems can consist of four or five teachers, including one who works as a speech therapist and perhaps one who is qualified as a psychologist and who undertakes counselling work.

The kind of work undertaken by the support teachers depends on the prevailing arrangements: in some cases their approach is basically to improve learning conditions for all pupils, but in other cases individual work is carried out with those having special needs.

The multiprofessional teams providing external support each operate in a geographical area which includes several schools. The average number of professionals is four, but it depends on the area they have to cover. The case studied for the OECD project belongs to the Basque Country Autonomous Community and here the multiprofessional teams are included in the local teachers' centres. This structure seems better able to facilitate and co-ordinate the different kinds of external support that ordinary and mainstream schools need.

The work that they do is focused on assessment of pupils, analysis and proposal of curriculum adaptations, counselling and school development activities.

Successful support systems for pupils with special educational needs

In the Spanish case studies report prepared for the OECD project[1] (OECD, 1995), we have described and evaluated examples of both issues, internal and external support, and we have analysed the factors which seem to be relevant to the relative success that some schools have had in integrating pupils with special educational needs.

Providing schools with new human resources, such as internal or external support, seems to be a necessary but not in itself sufficient requisite for an appropriate education for pupils with special educational needs in inclusive schools. Among factors conducive to success are the following:

- **active involvement and participation** of the whole teaching team, as well as of support staff, who are making decisions which affect pupils with special needs;

- **flexible** criteria for organising the support for pupils with special needs; that flexibility can only exists as the result of a **process** which entails:

- **clarity** in setting up procedures and ways of organising the support (both from internal and external viewpoints), its content and aim; clarity of criteria (which has not to be confused with inflexibility) has to exist for both teacher-tutors of pupils with special needs and pupils themselves;

- **continuous assessment** of support strategies to reinforce the adopted measures or to introduce those changes which best fit the pupil's requirements;

- **credibility**, which seems to stem not so much from deemed professional expertise, or from an appropriate level of satisfaction with the developed work, as from the support team's co-ordinated responsibility and effective functioning; and

- the existence within the schools of **school policy** which facilitates the support team's work at its various levels (organising, contents, evaluation).

---

1. Case studies No. 1 and No. 2 and their report preparation have been made by a team from the National Resource Centre for Special Education -- Ministry for Education and Science -- which was made up of Gerardo Echeita, Marian González and Camino Cadenas. Case study No. 3 and its report have been made by Rosa M. Murgia Quincoces, from the Curriculum Development Institute, Basque Country Autonomous Community.

There is enough evidence to confirm the appearance of these factors as resulting from a process, and not arising at random. Other "mediator" factors contributing to this process include the following:

- **positive attitudes to integration** that bear in mind special needs as a core component of the school system and not as a secondary consideration;

- **interdependency and personal relationships** that professionally respect disagreements;

- **efficient senior governing staff**, committed to meeting special needs;

- **a positive attitude when faced with uncertainty and difficulties**, resulting in co-ordinating strategies, professional co-operation and the implementing of in-service training as the best ways to achieve solutions; and,

- **administrative support**, whereby state and/or local education authorities consider these dimensions as positive factors to be reached in the schools and support them with resources and strategies to encourage school development in these directions.

Conclusion

These factors may have negative values. We may use them as a series of obstacles to overcome or steps which schools have adopted to overcome such difficulties. Strategies to overcome such difficulties can include the setting up of an "action plan" (Fullan, 1991a) through which good practice can be introduced progressively. It is self-evident that improving school integration processes is possible as an outcome of changes and adaptations to the general ongoing functioning of schools and on the curriculum which is offered to all pupils. That is, such improvement is a result of a deep "school reform" within the context of an "educational reform" in a very broad sense (UNESCO, 1994). All the actions designed to make these changes easier have to be considered as *prerequisites* for success in school integration.

The *social integration* of pupils with special needs is a long way from being optimal. The great goals still to reach are acceptance of the identities, understanding of their differences and recognition of their contribution to the group: not just a mere *assimilation* by the groups (OECD, 1994). It only will be possible to achieve full social integration if, at the same time, a culture of acceptance of and respect for differences is consolidated in our society. Inclusive schools seek to promote that culture and do not only attempt to change way schools work or the curriculum they provide.

CHAPTER 20

THE ROLE OF SPECIAL EDUCATION ARRANGEMENTS IN THE SHIFT TOWARDS LESS SEGREGATION IN THE NETHERLANDS

by

Aryan van der Leij

Introduction

In recent years, a major objective of policy on the education of pupils with special educational needs is the integration of these pupils into mainstream schools (OECD, 1995). Although the movement may be in the same general direction, the position, the pace and the pathways vary across countries. In this paper, the role of the special school and other special education arrangements in this process is discussed. I would like to argue that:

- it is more a matter of restricting segregation than of integration;
- the first aim of policy should be effective schooling and not integration per se; this aim includes adaptation of goal setting, instruction, practice and educational arrangements;
- the possibilities to adapt goal setting, instruction, practice and arrangements vary for different categories of handicap;
- the existence of separate special and ordinary schools hinders attempts to restrict segregation; and,
- integrated special education arrangements are beneficial to the restriction of segregation.

Restriction of segregation

Starting from the beginning of this century, many countries have executed a policy of providing special facilities outside ordinary schools or within the ordinary schools but outside regular classes. The idea of segregation is not confined to education. It has been the common policy in all kinds of areas where there are persons with special needs (*e.g.* because of age, of illness, of physical, sensory or mental handicaps, or of insanity). However, in recent years, the concept of segregation has been criticised. As is reviewed by Rispens (1994), the criticism is based on the assumption that it is easier to prepare a child with special needs to participate in society when the child is educated in the regular school instead of a special school, because the chance that the child will become a victim of (later) stigmatisation is smaller. Furthermore, the effects of special arrangements outside the regular school are not in line with the predictions of the underlying hypothesis of aptitude-treatment interaction: it is hard to prove that they produce better results than arrangements within the regular schools. Lastly, in most countries, the school system has been the subject of a large-scale process of reform, necessitated by major changes in societal demands and beliefs. Integration of pupils with special needs has been

137

included in a more general process of emancipation, also apparent in the integration of handicapped adults in the society. Instead of segregation, the concept of integration has been advocated as an alternative.

However, integration may not be the best description of what really needs to happen in education. Integration implies that the various parts have previously been separated. The question can be raised as to whether separation is necessary at all. According to modern beliefs, special needs thinking has to move away from deficit models and simple ideas about aptitude-treatment interaction in separate, permanent classrooms or special schools towards adaptive instruction models in mainstream classes and in temporary, goal-directed special classes. Restriction of segregation becomes the rule and segregation itself the exception. The concept of restriction of segregation does not contradict the view that a permanent stay in special education schools is a necessary arrangement for some, very handicapped, pupils. The emphasis, however, is on arrangements within the regular system. Recently, the concepts of "inclusion" and "inclusive education" have been proposed to cover this idea (*e.g.* by O'Hanlon, 1993).

Effective schooling

However, restriction of segregation should not be the only goal. In terms of formal regulations, it is easy to keep pupils with special educational needs in a mainstream class or ordinary school. The government only has to pass a law or other regulation prohibiting the exclusion of pupils from mainstream classes or ordinary schools, with the possible exception of those who are very handicapped. However, such legislation supplemented by sheer acceptance of disabled pupils is not sufficient. It would place the pupil with special educational needs in a tolerant but otherwise quite non-responsive environment with little prospect of beneficial development.

Restriction of segregation should be complemented by goal-oriented educational arrangements. The ultimate goal is not integration per se but that the pupil becomes proficient in various cognitive, affective and social skills. The specific goals may vary across and within the categories of pupils with special educational needs, but the main aim must be that pupils profit from their stay in an ordinary school. It should facilitate their participation in further schooling and life in the community (Ainscow, 1991).

An example may illustrate this point. In 1988, the Commission of the European Communities expressed doubt as to whether the educational systems of the highly industrialised countries of (western) Europe were successful in achieving the first goal of education: stimulation of literacy to be used as a tool in further schooling and everyday life ("functional literacy"). Many of the pupils were unable to read simple instructions or write short notes when they went to secondary schools. Estimates of at least 10 per cent were made, and various subcategories linked to different causes have been recognised. Most of these pupils were attending regular schools and could therefore be called "fully integrated" and "accepted". It was concluded that, in order to facilitate further schooling, pupils have to be educated in reading, spelling and writing according to their needs. Assuming that the situation has not improved significantly, guidelines for effective schooling can be given. Clear goals should be set and adaptive instruction methods should be used to arrive at a situation in which functional illiteracy really becomes an exception. The first priority is to improve mainstream arrangements. Emphasis on the principles of effective instruction and on extra time is a promising way to achieve this (Walberg, 1993). For some pupils, temporary special arrangements outside the ordinary classroom may be necessary additions. The routes may differ, but the minimal goals and effects -- achieving functional literacy to facilitate further schooling and development -- should be the same for all the pupils.

Variation across categories

When examples of integration are given, they tend to relate to the categories of pupils with severe disabilities such as mental retardation, Down's syndrome or autism (*e.g.* Müller, 1989). With regard to these pupils, the adaptation of goals is almost entirely restricted to the social domain. They may learn cognitive skills from a stimulating environment within a heterogeneous class, but the main point of their stay in the mainstream is to get along with other pupils, feel accepted and learn social skills which may facilitate their future development. In turn, the other pupils learn to get along with children who have major disabilities. For pupils with other obvious disabilities, *e.g.* blindness or physical impairment, goal setting is quite clear too. When they have learned to cope with their disabilities, and, in the case of the blind, mastered a compensating writing system, they can strive for the same proficiency in the cognitive skills as can pupils without disabilities.

Unfortunately, integration of other groups of pupils may be hard to accomplish. For instance, authors report that the regular system faces problems to accommodate severely handicapped pupils such as the deaf (Kyle, 1993) or the multiply handicapped (Appelhans, 1993). The picture of groups with specific or general learning disabilities and behavioural disorders is also still fuzzy. In their case, their disabilities and, consequently, the ways to adapt goals and instruction, are less obvious. Moreover, their difficulties are defined in relation to education and they appear in relatively large numbers. Inevitably, they are compared with pupils who share most of the characteristics (age, sex, intelligence, background) but lack the learning disability. For that reason, the teacher has more difficulty in understanding their needs and may be less willing to cope with their problems than with the obvious problems of physical, sensory or mental disability. In my opinion, supported by authors like Williams (1993), the test of effective restriction of segregation is not the inclusion of the occasional handicapped pupil in the regular school, but the success of adapting the regular system to the needs of pupils, without obvious disabilities, who tend to disrupt that system because of their need for intensive instruction, practice and behaviour modification.

Conservatism by separation

The conservatism of the ordinary schools may be an obstacle to effective mainstream schooling. Schools show conservatism in two ways (Reynolds, 1991). One is to repel outside influence which may expose the school and its inadequacy. It is, to a certain degree, a defensive apparatus that is unwilling to take the risks necessitated by potentially changing organisational practices. The other is to preserve what is already there, not in a defensive way but offensively. What is done is valued highly and poor conditions are blamed for what cannot be done. Support systems can cope with this conservatism as long as they receive the extra funds needed. Unfortunately, funding may be insufficient during the process of innovation. Moreover, most extra funding stops at the end of a project, leaving the schools with the task of continuing alone. When extra support does not succeed in incorporating special instructional skills and strategies into the daily routines of teachers, the effect of that extra support will fade away once the project comes to an end. However, this is not an easy job. Ordinary schools need to develop into flexible, collaborative institutions with an extensive problem-solving capacity, and the teachers have to adopt adaptive teaching methods in heterogeneous classes. Furthermore, not only the pupils, but also the system of regular and special education arrangements needs to be integrated. Specialists like special needs teachers and resource teachers (internal supportive systems) may stimulate this process but only when their efforts are focused both on the pupils with special educational needs and on the teacher of the mainstream classroom.

Special schools, too, may be an obstacle in the process of integrating pupils with special educational needs in ordinary schools. It is a well-known fact that segregative arrangements like special schools tend to attract more and more pupils, thereby making themselves indispensable. This is an interactive process: ordinary schools use special schools to get rid of their most difficult pupils and special schools encourage the ordinary schools to send them. The pupil is transferred and little or no communication follows: the responsibility is transferred with the pupil. As long as ordinary and special schools legally co-exist as two independent systems, it will be hard to restrict the segregation of pupils with special educational needs. Parents can even go to court to claim the right of their child to be sent to a special school. Legislation that regulates ordinary and special schools within one framework, restricting the flow of pupils from one to the other, seems to be the first prerequisite for the restriction of segregation (Saulle, 1994, cited by Meijer, 1995). Moreover, the idea of shared responsibility should be furthered by reinforcing relations between special and ordinary schools at all levels (administration, curriculum, teaching staff, specialists). Although their first reaction may be one of conservatism too -- a desire to leave the status quo as it is -- special schools should support the idea of shared responsibility.

Integrative special arrangements

In general, the status of integration of pupils with disabilities in the regular system may be considered as an indication of the adaptive power of that system. However, even when mainstream classroom management is optimal, supplementary special arrangements outside the regular classroom may be necessary to fulfil the needs of some of the pupils. It is clear that in addition to mainstreaming and education in special schools, various intermediate arrangements have been developed. To define the ways to organise integrative arrangements in a more specific way, Hegarty's paper of 1989 is paraphrased.

Label	*Short description*
special school throughout and permanently	*"segregation to another school"*
special school throughout and temporary	*"segregation and placing back"*
special school base and mainstream school part-time	*"shuttling between special and regular school"*
special unit/class throughout	*"segregated within regular school"*
special unit/class base, attending mainstream classes part-time	*"shuttling between special and regular class"*
mainstream school base and special school part-time	*"shuttling between regular and special school"*
mainstream base, attending special unit/class part-time	*"shuttling between regular and special class"*
mainstream placement and withdrawal for specialist teaching	*"regular class and remedial teaching"*
mainstream placement with extra educational support	*"help within the class"*

The movement towards restriction of segregation is demonstrated while reading the list from top to bottom. All the models except the first two assume the physical proximity of ordinary and special provision which facilitates shared responsibility. Member countries of the OECD have adopted different positions in the list. For example, in Italy and Sweden relatively few pupils are registered as having special needs (0-3 per cent) and only 0-1 per cent receive education in completely segregated schools or classes. In contrast, in The Netherlands 4-7 per cent of the pupils are registered and more than 2 per cent attend special schools (percentages of the total population aged 6 to 17; figures cited from Pijl and Meijer, 1994, pp. 118-119). Unfortunately for policy makers, it is hard to tell which arrangement is the most effective. Some authors are inclined to accept that effectiveness is not the issue or even a non-issue because of "untestability": *"Controversy (...) will continue and will not be abated by any amount of scientific inquiry. The controversy is based on differences in faith, experience, and values, and the relative validity of the different positions is untestable"* (Landesman and Butterfield, 1987, p. 814, cited by Rispens, 1994). As an important methodological constraint, lack of experimental control -- the groups of pupils placed in different arrangements are never well matched on relevant variables -- reduces the validity of the research data (Hegarty, 1993). Nevertheless, the general belief seems to be that positions at the bottom of the list are preferable to positions at the top, at least for pupils who do not have severe disabilities. The least that can be said to support this belief is lack of evidence that the segregated system is better, in which case non-empirical reasons like the negative perception of stigmatisation and the higher costs make the difference (Meijer, 1995).

As a consequence, the role of special education arrangements in the shift towards less segregation may be expressed by three principles.

First, special education should develop into a highly flexible system of specialist support and help that is fully integrated with the ordinary school system to create a flexible education system with a high capacity of problem solving and shared responsibility. Internal and external supportive systems are needed to support the teacher of the mainstream class. It is important to create a climate conducive to learning based on common conceptual frameworks and shared beliefs. Possibly the most important belief is that heterogeneity should prevail, wherever this is possible and beneficial to all.

Second, special arrangements of some sort continue to be necessary within the ordinary school. It would be very unwise to assume that non-segregation is completed when the ordinary school is turned into a tolerant locus of education. As I argued before, pupils with various disabilities not only have the right to be accepted but also to be taught properly, at least in the basic skills. Although some may be helped within the ordinary classroom, many need special attention and extra time in small groups. The groups may be run by specialists in remedial teaching and other therapies. As an alternative, the model of multiple teachers in the class may be efficient ("tutors").

Third, beside providing permanent education to pupils with severe disabilities, special schools as part of the supportive system should specialise in early, goal-directed intervention for short periods. The earlier intervention starts, the higher the chance that it is effective, as studies on the instruction of prereading skills show (Bradley and Bryant, 1985; Lundberg *et al.*, 1988).

In addition to the arrangements, the qualifications of the ordinary teacher, the special teacher and other specialists need to be part of the innovative agenda (Hegarty, 1994). The expertise of special needs teachers and other specialists should be incorporated in initial and in-service training.

CHAPTER 21

REMEDIAL TUITION IN THE ORDINARY CLASS FOR PUPILS WITH LEARNING DIFFICULTIES IN SWITZERLAND

by

Gérard Bless

Ordinary classes with remedial tuition for pupils with learning difficulties

In Switzerland, pupils with severe learning difficulties traditionally are separated from the ordinary school system and schooled in self-contained special classes. Yet over the past ten years an undeniable tendency can be observed. Particularly in sparsely populated areas of the country, a great number of the regional school administrations tend to integrate pupils with learning difficulties into the ordinary classes. The most popular way of such integration is the schooling in "ordinary classes with remedial tuition" (Bless, 1995, pp. 61-63). The following diagram encapsulates the arrangement.

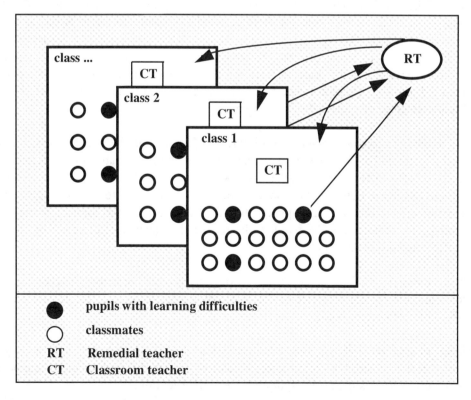

●	pupils with learning difficulties
○	classmates
RT	Remedial teacher
CT	Classroom teacher

These classes are organised and managed in the same way as the conventional ordinary classes and they are provided with the same infrastructure (speech therapy, school psychology, psychomotor therapy etc.). They count an average of 19 pupils. To support the pupils with learning difficulties, the school provides a remedial teacher as well as the usual infrastructure. This special teacher works in different classes in close co-operation with the classroom teachers. Depending on the geographical circumstances he/she works in different schools and/or different communities.

As for the degree of integration, it is important to know that in the first place the "ordinary class with remedial tuition" has been conceived for children who are traditionally assigned to self-contained special classes due to their notable learning difficulties. Therefore it is more appropriate to consider the "ordinary class with remedial tuition" as a school structure which helps to reduce segregation rather than to talk about true integration. The concept of this school structure is still based on the idea of "integratable" vs. "non-integratable" children as the "ordinary class with remedial tuition" is only designed for pupils suffering from moderate degrees of disability. Up to now children with severe disability are still excluded from integration into "ordinary classes with remedial tuition"; they are still assigned to self-contained classes in special institutions.

The role of remedial teaching

With regard to integrative settings it is more appropriate to talk about the "role of remedial teaching" and of "remedial teachers" than about the "roles of the special school", as this term is linked to segregative institutions. The following roles can be identified:

– *Individual remedial tuition.* Generally the classroom teacher is not able to give individual support to each pupil with learning difficulties. For that reason, the teacher can ask for the assistance of a remedial teacher. During 2 to 6 lessons a week, pupils with learning difficulties can benefit from individual support, special therapies and remedial tuition in addition to the regular classroom instruction. Remedial tuition is granted according to the special needs of a child, either individually or in small groups. If possible it should take place during ordinary classes within the classroom. If the concept does not allow remedial tuition in the classroom, the pupils concerned join the remedial teacher in a resource room outside the class, where they receive individual assistance or remedial tuition in small groups.

– *Educational guidance for classroom teachers and parents.* In addition, the remedial teacher acts as an educational consultant for the classroom teachers as well as for the parents of children with learning difficulties. The information, suggestions and advice of the remedial teacher often allow the classroom teacher to determine the specific needs of each pupil, to choose and to apply the most appropriate educational and therapeutic measures and to integrate them into the daily classroom teaching. By counselling the parents, the remedial teacher tries to sensitise them to the child's specific educational situation.

– *Prevention in the classroom.* The close co-operation between the remedial teacher and the classroom teacher and the regular presence of the remedial teacher in the classroom may prevent the learning difficulties of certain pupils.

– *Observation and diagnostic.* Each individualised educational setting requires a regular observation and -- in the sense of a continuous evaluation -- a careful and accurate diagnostic procedure which has to serve as the basis of all pedagogic intervention.

- *Co-ordination.* The remedial teacher also acts as a co-ordinator between the many other specialists (speech therapist, school psychologist, psychomotor specialists, etc.) who are involved with a child who needs special assistance.

For a more detailed description of the role of the remedial teacher within an integrative school setting, see Bless (1995, pp. 57-61, 64-68).

The extent and the duration of remedial tuition vary according to the needs of each pupil. The practical organisation and realisation basically depend on the personality of the remedial teacher on the one hand and on the degree of co-operation of the classroom teacher on the other hand. Depending on the place and the people concerned, the procedure may vary considerably.

Considering the multiple responsibilities and functions of a remedial teacher, this job asks for a strong personality endowed with a sense of co-operation as well as with a profound professional knowledge. A remedial teacher with little practical experience who does not constantly improve his/her knowledge will not be able to offer more than repetitive lessons to the pupils, which is neither in accordance with the needs of the pupils concerned nor with the concept of remedial tuition.

Extending the ordinary class by including remedial teaching requires various modifications in the fields of activities of the different professionals involved. The close co-operation with the remedial teacher leads to supplementary work for the classroom teacher and to fundamental changes in the fields of activities of the whole teaching staff of ordinary classes. Yet most of the teachers consider these changes as a challenging and positive experience. On the other hand the experiences with integrative forms of schooling seem to disclose some problems of delimitation concerning the fields of activities of the remedial teacher and the school psychologist, problems which are still waiting to be resolved (Niedermann, Bless and Sassenroth, 1992).

The efficacy of the "ordinary class with remedial tuition"

The role of remedial teaching within this integrative school setting can only be estimated by taking into account the impact of this form of schooling on the development of the pupils concerned. The following statements result from various longitudinal researches on the effect of integrative schooling on pupils with learning difficulties (Haeberlin *et al.,* 1991; Bless, 1995). These studies did compare pupils with learning difficulties who were integrated into "ordinary classes with remedial tuition" with similar pupils in self-contained special classes.

The following observations can be considered as positive aspects:

- *Maintenance of the social roots of the child.* The "ordinary class with remedial tuition" to a large extent prevents social uprooting from the place of residence of the pupils with all its consequences (for instance the impoverishment of social contacts with children of the same age living in the same village). In self-contained special classes one child in three has to leave his/her place of residence every day to attend school in a neighbouring village. "Ordinary classes with remedial tuition" help to reduce this rate to one pupil in twenty-five.

- *Attitude towards school.* Compared to segregation, the integration of pupils with learning difficulties does not change their attitude towards school.

– *Development of school performances.* In "ordinary classes with remedial tuition", pupils with learning difficulties make clearly more progress than comparable pupils in self-contained special classes.

– *Development of gifted pupils.* There are no indications that the development of pupils identified as gifted is impeded by the integration of pupils with learning difficulties.

– *Economic aspects.* A comparison of the cost per pupil with learning difficulties shows that the integration into a "ordinary class with remedial tuition" does not increase the cost of schooling. Therefore the economic aspect can be neglected in favour of the educational aspects.

The following observations can be considered a priori as negative aspects:

– *Social status of pupils with learning difficulties.* Pupils with learning difficulties in "ordinary classes with remedial tuition" have a lower social status than their classmates. Besides, the self-assessment of their social relations within the class is less favourable than the self-assessment of their peers. Yet the problem of social isolation of integrated pupils cannot be solved by removing them to a self-contained special class, as in those classes the same mechanisms as in "ordinary classes with remedial tuition" seem to determine the degree of popularity. For that reason, this aspect seems to be a priori unfavourable.

– *Self-concept with regard to the educational and intellectual capacities.* Pupils with learning difficulties in "ordinary classes with remedial tuition" assess their self-concept with regard to their own educational and intellectual capacities lower than pupils in self-contained special classes. Yet this self-assessment seems to be appropriate, as integrated pupils have to compare themselves with pupils of different intellectual levels whereas pupils in self-contained special classes can compare themselves with their classmates who also suffer from learning difficulties. Consequently, the self-concept of integrated pupils can be considered as very realistic, as they are in fact weaker than their classmates.

Conclusion

Beyond all doubt, the research outcomes mentioned above as well as the positive attitude expressed by the participants of various inquiries indicate that remedial teaching within the scope of the "ordinary class with remedial tuition" is a valuable pedagogical practice. No doubt, this school model and its methods of teaching can be considered as a valuable alternative to the self-contained special class for pupils with learning difficulties.

However, one key problem of school structures which practise a partial integration only for certain categories of handicapped children -- *e.g.* the "ordinary class with remedial tuition" -- has to be emphasised yet. On the one hand, one of the most important objectives of integration policy is to adapt the educational goals, on the other hand this adaptation becomes quite difficult with regard to the integration of pupils with learning difficulties. This conflict becomes evident in the "ordinary class with remedial tuition". Individualisation on the level of teaching has more or less been realised; individualisation at the level of educational goals and of the pupils' evaluation still waits for realisation. Daily practice shows that this school model is not tolerant enough, because certain pupils do not achieve the goals, which have been established for all pupils. The following reasons are responsible for this lack of adaptation:

– On the one hand this school model has been created for pragmatic reasons (as an alternative to residential schools for pupils with learning difficulties). The establishment of "ordinary classes with remedial tuition" has not been the result of serious discussion concerning the idea of integration; such discussion never really happened on a serious, thorough level, neither on the initiative of the responsible authorities nor on the initiative of the parents and the teachers. To stand up for integration inevitably means to stand up for diversity and variety, which is not the case in "ordinary classes with remedial tuition".

On the other hand, the adaptation of educational goals cannot be realised uncompromisingly as long as integration continues to be only partial integration and as long as children who suffer from more severe disabilities are excluded from ordinary schools. A more extensive heterogeneity of the classes should entail a more extensive individualisation at the level of goals as well as at the level of pupils' evaluation. This should also lead to an increase of tolerance face to face with human diversity.

Part V

ACCOUNTABILITY AND FUNDING

CHAPTER 22

THE NATIONAL CURRICULUM, EDUCATIONAL STANDARDS AND THE LOCAL MANAGEMENT OF ENGLISH SCHOOLS

by

Klaus Wedell

Introduction

I have been asked to consider the "reforms" brought about by recent education legislation in the UK as an instance of the impact which systemic changes may have on the development of inclusive education.

At the outset, it is important to note that, in discussing "inclusion", we are considering a development beyond "integration". Integration has the implication of bringing pupils with special educational needs *into* the prevailing mainstream educational provision. Inclusion, by contrast, implies that pupils with special educational needs start and remain in mainstream provision. In other words, inclusion starts from the assumption that educational provision has to be geared to meet the needs of pupils in all their diversity, including "special educational needs". This point emerged clearly from the UNESCO World Conference on special needs education, held in Salamanca in 1994. The Statement which was issued from that Conference (UNESCO, 1994) affirmed:

"(...) the necessity and urgency of providing education for children, youth an adults with special educational needs within the regular education system. Regular schools with this inclusive orientation provide an effective education to the majority of children and improve the efficiency and ultimately cost-effectiveness of the entire education system".

This is a bold assertion, but the size of the step from "integration" to "inclusion" may not have been fully grasped even by those drawing up the Statement. Inclusion requires the re-conceptualisation of conventional education systems, so that they can promote the progress of all pupils. Some writers (*e.g.* Ainscow, 1995) have suggested that inclusion can be achieved mainly by a change of attitude among teachers, so that they are willing to make modifications to their teaching and to the way they respond to pupils in their classes. While these kinds of changes are clearly in the right direction, it seems unlikely that they will be sufficient to achieve the outcomes implied by the Salamanca Statement.

In a recent OECD review of the literature on how the *integration* of pupils with special educational needs actually supported their achievement, Hegarty summarised the findings as showing that:

"the conclusions were tentative at best, and generally inconclusive" (Hegarty, 1993).

And yet such a conclusion is hardly surprising. Elsewhere (Wedell, 1995) I have commented:

"one is seeking the right for pupils with special educational needs to be included in educational environments which are predicated on misconceived assumptions about the homogeneity of pupils' learning needs".

The assumptions of homogeneity occur not only across pupil diversity. More importantly, these assumptions do not allow for the various ways in which the learning demands of different aspects of the curriculum interact with pupil diversity. The nature and size of pupil groupings tend to be rigid, and not flexible in order to respond to these variations in learning need. At the most, groupings are arranged on one particular criterion such as "ability" or achievement level. It is well-known that grouping on one dimension invariably leaves diversity in another such as motivation or persistence, which may be just as relevant to educational outcomes. "Setting" pupils by subject cannot achieve the degree of flexibility which diversity in learning needs demands, and considerations about flexibility of grouping to meet learning needs cannot, in themselves, deal with how the social aims of education can be met.

In most education systems, the size of groupings is in any case more likely to be determined by economy of scale (dividing the number of pupils by the number of available teachers) rather than by the particular learning demands of the aspect of the curriculum taught.

In other words, the limited benefits of integration for pupils with special educational needs derive from the fact that provision for these pupils at best is seen as requiring some modifications to standard educational approaches. These standard educational approaches require teachers to deliver a standard curriculum to pupils in classes of standard sizes. These "standard" approaches force teachers into targeting their teaching at the average levels of their pupils, as though there was a homogeneity in their pupils' learning needs. Teachers know full well that the most obvious point about their pupils is that they are all different -- that they represent a diversity of learning needs. This has been put well by Slavin (1987):

"Perhaps the most difficult problem of class organisation is dealing with the fact that students come into the class with different levels of knowledge, skills and learning rate and motivation. Teachers can always be sure that if they teach one lesson to a whole class, some students will learn more quickly than others. Some students may not learn the lesson at all..." (p. 159).

The result is that pupils with high achievement, so long as they are motivated, use their abilities to derive what benefit they can from the teaching offered, while pupils with difficulties in learning cling on to their teacher's differentiated help as best they can, or give up as they fall further behind.

The limitations of education systems in meeting the diversity of pupils' learning needs is illustrated in findings from another study from the OECD Centre for Research and Innovation, of children and youth at risk (OECD, 1995). This confirmed the scale of the problem. The study defined "risk" as "failure to integrate into a normally acceptable pattern of social responsibility, particularly with regard to work and family life". The estimates of the "at risk" pupil population in the participating countries ranged between 15 per cent and 30 per cent of the age group. Clearly, this kind of finding shows that the economy of scale in deploying the teaching force results in a serious wastage rate for pupil outcomes. This in turn raises questions about the validity of the criteria on which the economy of scale is evaluated in the first place.

However, a line of argument such as the above leaves one with the onus of weighing up the cost benefit and other implications of education systems which could be responsive to the demands of inclusion. Not that the Salamanca Statement needs to be justified in cost benefit terms alone, although its wording inclines that way. The starting point for meeting pupil diversity is illustrated in the following figure:

Figure 1: **Matrix 1.**

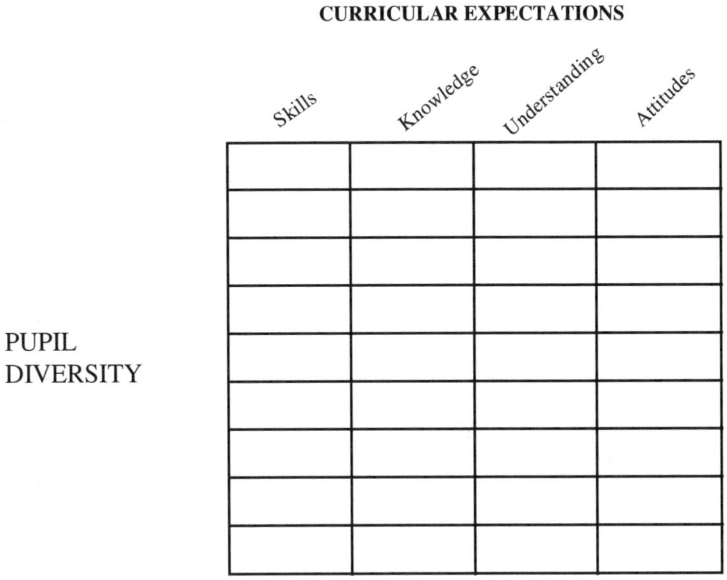

CURRICULAR EXPECTATIONS

	Skills	Knowledge	Understanding	Attitudes
PUPIL DIVERSITY				

This figure represents pupil diversity in learning need in the vertical dimension, and links this with the demands made by a curriculum in the horizontal dimension. Curriculum is here taken in the broad sense of the aims which a society requires its education system to fulfil. Each cell then represents the challenge to match the demands of the particular curricular content to the particular learning needs of individual pupils. Inclusion implies that schools take ownership of this challenge, within an overall commitment to equality of educational opportunity. It is interesting to note that current studies of "school effectiveness" and "school improvement" (*e.g.* Sammons *et al.,* 1994) usually do not fully acknowledge the complexity implied by this matrix, since they tend to focus primarily on modifying school management and teacher involvement *within* the conventional patterns of school organisation. Indeed, it is acknowledged that this area of research has not resolved the issue of the criteria which should be applied.

In this paper I want to look at some of the recent legislative changes in the English education system, as they impinge on the attempts at progress towards inclusive education for pupils with special educational needs. In conclusion, I will then consider the potential for meeting some of the implications of Matrix One within current educational practices.

The English education system and recent legislation

It is necessary first to place the recent education legislation in the context of the education system in England, before dealing with the consequences of the legislation for pupils with special educational needs.

For the sake of conciseness, I will consider the recent legislation in the English education system in relation to Matrix Two, shown in Figure 2.

Figure 2: Matrix 2.

CURRICULAR AND ASSESSMENT SPECIFICATIONS

	National	Local	School
School systems			
Schools			
Classes			

EDUCATION SYSTEM

This refers in a simplistic way to the education systems of most countries. The vertical dimension shows the education system organised into school systems, schools and classes, and the curriculum and its assessment determined at national, local and school levels. In general, over the last 30 years public education in England has attempted to accommodate pupil diversity by organising pupil grouping mainly by age at both primary and secondary levels within the principles of comprehensive education. However, pupils with the more marked forms of special needs have been served in special schools or units attached to mainstream schools.

The English education system differed from that in most other countries, in that the curriculum offered in schools was largely determined at the local level by Local Education Authorities (LEAs) and at the level of individual schools. External assessment of pupils' achievement above the local level did not occur before the end of the compulsory school age of 16, and was mainly directed at pupils of average or above average attainment. These examinations were organised by independent agencies. A significant proportion of pupils left school without taking any form of final examination.

Until the late 1980s, the most important development in educational provision for pupils with special educational needs was the Warnock Report on this topic (1978). This, in turn, led to the 1981 Education Act which came into force in 1983. In principle the Act promoted the integration of pupils with special educational needs, but qualified this in relation to practical and economic considerations. It also promoted better support for those 18 per cent or so of pupils with special educational needs who were already in mainstream schools. The Act led to a general tendency for pupils (other than those with more severe emotional and behaviour problems) increasingly to be educated in ordinary schools (Goacher *et al.,* 1988). The Act placed responsibility on LEAs to increase the services supporting pupils with special educational needs in mainstream schools, and to encourage schools to employ support staff themselves. The Act also introduced a means whereby LEAs allocated additional resources individually to around 2 per cent of pupils with more severe special educational needs on the basis of a multiprofessional assessment of their special needs (the Statement procedure). Increasingly these pupils also had their needs met in mainstream schools.

The aim of these forms of support for pupils and also for teachers were to increase teachers' capacity to incorporate pupils with special educational needs in mainstream classes. However, the extent to which this was achieved varied greatly for the reasons mentioned by Slavin cited above. Schools differed in their organisation of special needs support. Over the years there was a decreasing tendency for pupils to be withdrawn from their class by advisory and support teachers for individual or small group help. Help was more often offered indirectly through teacher consultation and advice, or pupils were directly supported within their mainstream classes (Ireson and Evans, 1995).

The 1981 Act was brought in by the current administration. From 1988 onwards, the same administration embarked on a series of new Education Acts. The new legislation originated from a concern that the prevailing education system was felt not to be producing adequate educational standards across a consistent curricular coverage. The solution proposed was to raise standards by explicitly imposing market forces on the provision of education -- although these forces had, to some degree, long existed implicitly (Fish and Evans, 1995). The then Secretary of State for Education was proud to claim that his legislation introduced competition between schools. The legislation made most of the funding for schools directly dependent on pupil numbers. It also introduced a detailed national system of assessing pupils' achievement within the framework of a newly formulated National Curriculum. The National Curriculum was the first to be introduced in England. It covered ten subjects at ten levels across the compulsory school age of five to sixteen. The legislation gave all pupils an entitlement to be taught this curriculum. The assessment of pupils' achievement in this curriculum could then enable parents, if they wished, to choose those schools which produced the highest average achievement. For this purpose, the legislation also provided for the information about pupils' average achievement in each school to be publicised in league tables.

The legislation forced LEAs to pass most of their funds directly on to the schools in their areas. The aim was to give schools increased autonomy in deciding how to spend their available finances. However, the funding formula was also intended to include a small element to cover pupils' special educational needs, although it was recommended that this element should be determined by the proxy indicator of the proportion of pupils receiving free school meals. Schools were also encouraged to "opt out" of their LEA systems altogether, and to place themselves under a central funding agency, which enabled them potentially to receive enhanced funding. LEAs had their funding reduced in proportion to the proportion of their schools which "opted out".

The series of Education Acts has continued over subsequent years. During these years, there have been increasing national financial constraints, which are having a number of consequences for schools, including a reduction in teacher staffing which is partially coinciding with a gradual upturn in pupil numbers. As a consequence, class sizes are becoming larger. The administration claims that there is no evidence why this should impinge on the quality of education offered. Educational statistics over the years since the recent legislation started have in general, indicated a rise in standards. However, doubt has then tended to be cast on these findings, because it is felt that assessment was becoming more lenient.

The curriculum assessment system has been gradually reduced, because it was found to be impracticable. The National Curriculum has been found to be over-prescriptive and partly unworkable, and so has also been reduced. However, it is interesting to note that, among those teachers who are choosing to retire early, the proportion doing so for health reasons is reported to have risen from 16 per cent in 1988/9, to almost 25 per cent in 1993/4 (*Times Educational Supplement*, 1995).

LEAs have been required to increase from 85 per cent to 90 per cent the proportion of their funds which they pass on to schools, but a subsequent move to increase this percentage still further has up to now been abandoned. Most recently, legislation is being considered, which would allow schools to admit up to 15 per cent of their pupils through selection by interview, but it is not clear how this is intended to match the underlying "market forces" principle of parental choice.

The impact of recent legislation on the education of pupils with special educational needs

It is interesting to note, that in principle, many of the aspects of the recent educational legislation could have made a positive contribution to schools' capacity to meet the diversity of their pupils' learning needs.

The National Curriculum, although it was widely criticised for its narrow focus on ten subjects, was introduced as an *entitlement* for all pupils. In principle, this entitlement therefore could safeguard the breadth of education offered to pupils with special educational needs. The legislation does allow for parts or all of the curriculum (and its assessment) to be "modified" or "disapplied", if it is not found to be appropriate for a particular pupil. However, such a step (unless it is temporary) can only be taken after a formal procedure. Such a procedure, while in principle having a safeguarding function, in practice militates against an inclusive ethos.

The National Curriculum is formulated in terms of a continuum of ten levels to cover the compulsory school age from 5-16. As a result, it offers all teachers for the first time a comprehensive view of the progression of the curriculum. This could enable teachers to match their teaching to the particular achievement of any pupil in their class. The curriculum designers also provided suggestions about how teaching approaches could be modified to meet the needs of pupils with sensory or motor disabilities (NCC, 1989). Not surprisingly it has proved more difficult to offer teachers advice on how to modify teaching and content for pupils whose main difficulty is in learning, and who achieve well below the average expected for their age. The National Curriculum starts at the level expected of 5 year olds. Attempts have been made to formulate downwards extensions of the subjects, but this has raised questions about the meaningfulness of "subjects" at these levels. Recently, the National Foundation for Educational Research has been asked to explore ways in which the progress of pupils can be assessed, when pupils' slow progress requires a "small steps" approach either within or below the range of the National Curriculum.

Unfortunately, given the onus of competition between schools in terms of aggregate achievement levels, and the increasingly constrained resources and larger class sizes, teachers are forced into the well-known dilemma about how to produce good class results:

"Teachers, whether in regular or special class environments, cannot escape the necessary choice between higher means (*i.e.* maximising mean performance of the group by concentrating resources on the most able learners) and narrowing variances (*i.e.* minimising the variance in performance of the group by concentrating resources on the least able learners) as long as resources are scarce and students differ." (Gerber and Semmel, 1985).

This conflict was recognised by the administration, who, as mentioned above, allowed the requirement for all pupils to be assessed to be "modified or disapplied" for individual pupils, including those who had special educational needs. The official document (DES, 1989) explains that by "disapplying" a pupil from assessment in the national curriculum, a school can avoid that pupil's poor achievement lowering the school's average standing in the league tables. This illustrates how the need to produce competitive aggregate achievement levels could leave teachers with no option but to marginalise pupils with special educational needs.

An aspect of the legislation which was potentially helpful for pupils with special educational needs was the increased delegation of funds from LEAs to schools. In principle, schools *could* have greater scope to use their funds to meet their particular circumstances, including the need to allocate resources to meet pupils' special educational needs. Schools do, in fact, do this. Indeed, a study by Lunt *et al.* (1994) found that in several parts of the country schools which were near each other, were pooling funds to share resources (including staff) to support their pupils with special educational needs. However, a recent follow-up study suggests that the increasingly limited funds available to schools are making the sharing of staff difficult.

Wedell (1993) summarised the findings from a number of studies carried out following the 1988 Act. Studies carried out between 1990 and 1992 showed, for example, that:

- 85 per cent of a sample of secondary teachers were concerned about the resources for pupils with special educational needs;
- there was an increase in the number of pupils for whom schools sought additional resources through the Statement procedure; and,
- the then Department for Education expressed concern about the number of pupils who were excluded from schools because of disturbing behaviour.

Another consequence of the reduced funding which LEAs were allowed to retain, was that LEAs generally reduced their special needs advisory and support services. Some discontinued their ownership of the services, and forced them to maintain themselves by selling their services to schools. Again, it might be argued that, in principle, this would force services to be effective and to make sure that they offered what schools needed. This expediency might operate with services for the more prevalent forms of special educational needs. It is less practical for services for minority special needs such as hearing and visual impairment, which for that reason are more costly to maintain. These services can easily disappear with the vagaries of market forces, and are then difficult to revive.

By the time the proposals for the 1993 education legislation became known, around 140 parent and professional associations grouped themselves into the "Special Educational Consortium", to lobby parliament on behalf of pupils with special educational needs. The 1993 Act promoted the "opting out" of schools and the reduction of LEAs' responsibilities. The Consortium was particularly concerned that the Act did not address the 18 per cent or so of pupils with special educational needs in mainstream schools within these changes. The Act took away the LEAs' co-ordinating role both for special educational support across the range of special educational needs and for the integration of health and other services with the education service. Co-ordination was left to the goodwill of parties concerned.

The Consortium failed to change the terms of the Act on this and a number of other points, although some concerns were addressed in recommendations in the official Circulars following the legislation. Largely as a consequence of the lobby, the administration extended the coverage of a part of the Act dealing with the Statement Procedure. This became the Code of Practice on the Identification and Assessment of Special Educational Needs (DFE, 1994). Lengthy discussions between members of the Consortium and officials resulted in the content of the Code being extended to cover pupils without Statements. The Code requires that all schools should have a policy for supporting their pupils with special educational needs. Schools are also required to appoint a member of staff to act as a Special Educational Needs Co-ordinator (SENCO), to advise and support teachers in identifying and meeting pupils' special educational needs. The Code sets out a sequence of stages for seeking additional support for a pupil, and links this with monitoring the pupil's progress. One aim of these stages is to ensure that the school has made an effort to help a pupil, before it seeks help from the LEA through the Statement procedure.

It will be evident that the formulation of the Code is a long way from an inclusive policy, but at least it firmly places on schools the responsibility for acting to meet their pupils' special educational needs. The legal status of the Code is somewhat unclear. However, the Code forms part of the criteria on which schools are inspected. Responsibility for these inspections was taken away from LEAs in one of the previous education Acts in this series. Independent teams are now invited to put in tenders for this task to the newly formed Office for Standards in Education (OFSTED), derived from the reduced service of Her Majesty's Inspectors. Unfortunately, it has been difficult for these teams to recruit specialists in special educational needs.

A recent survey in 33 LEAs carried out by HMI from OFSTED (1996) found that less than half of SENCOs in primary, and a third of SENCOs in secondary schools had any form of special needs qualification. Preliminary findings from a survey by the National Confederation of Parent Teacher Associations found that 60 per cent of 1 100 primary and secondary schools reported that they had difficulty in meeting the requirements of the Code within their current budgets (NCPTA, 1996). A study (Lewis, 1995) of primary schools, reported that about 30 per cent of SENCOs were not allocated any time to carry out their SENCO duties on top of their full-time teaching load, and a further 30 per cent had one hour or less a week.

It will be evident from the above, that the recent education legislation in England has, in principle, offered some opportunities for moves to more inclusive education for pupils with special educational needs. However the overriding market economy ethos repeatedly made it difficult to implement the provisions of the legislation in ways which were positive for these pupils. Even those schools which were inclined towards inclusive approaches found, in the face of the market pressures, that their scope was curtailed by the downward spiral of allocated funding. One should also not underestimate the demoralising effect on schools and their staffs of the continual criticisms of the teaching profession engendered by the administration. In the midst of all this, there are of course, many schools where the leadership and mutual support among staff have maintained morale, even in those schools whose achievements for pupils with special educational needs have not been recognised by their standing in the league tables.

The implications of inclusion

Although the English education system has currently been rendered far from ready to implement inclusive education, it may be relevant in conclusion to consider some aspects of educational organisation and practice which could contribute to such a development.

It is clear that the implementation of inclusion is incompatible with the current practicalities of meeting pupils' diverse needs in schools. The current system forces an inflexibility of pupil groupings, which in turn engenders exclusionary consequences for pupils with special educational needs. The Matrix One indicates the degree of flexibility needed if pupil diversity and the varied demands of the curriculum are to be met. What therefore is required is firstly, a decoupling of the practical measures for meeting pupils' individual learning needs from the exclusionary associations which they currently engender. Secondly, there is a need to realise the potential of existing resources to support teaching and learning, which is at least within range of economic possibilities. Thirdly, such a system has to be implemented within an organisational unit, to which an individual pupil can *belong*, and which in turn, can take responsibility for that pupil.

Starting with the third requirement, which underlies the implementation of inclusion, there are instances in England of secondary schools which have set themselves to meet such a requirement. For example, there is a secondary school into which a previously separate special school has been incorporated. There are also clusters of schools -- within the primary and the secondary phase, and across phases, which collaborate to take responsibility for meeting their pupils' special educational needs (Lunt *et al.*, 1994). There are also special schools which have linked with mainstream schools in order to serve the range of their pupils. These are all instances of ways in which schools share a joint commitment to meet the diversity of their pupils' learning needs. The pooling of their available resources is an instance of the way in which their value can be enhanced -- with reference to the above second requirement. The collaboration to meet pupils' special educational needs has in some instances extended beyond the education services, to involving the health and social services, and the voluntary agencies.

The first requirement mentioned above is perhaps the one which affects the individual pupil's experience most directly. As already indicated, this relates to the way in which the teaching-learning approaches themselves reflect the aims of inclusion. The overall curricular aim of inclusion has been realised through the extent to which individual pupils can feel members of a group. Such a group has not only to be one in which each member can learn to value the other, regardless of the diversity of learning needs, but also one in which they feel the teacher feels an equal responsibility towards each member. In the present education system, in principle such groups may be found in secondary schools which have mixed-ability tutor groups, and in ordinary classes in many primary schools, where they are sometimes called a "home-base". In secondary schools tutor groups are rarely given the curricular status required by the point made here. If the full status were to be achieved at both the primary and the secondary phase, the system would need to give the teacher the central responsibility for monitoring and supporting the pupil's progress, and thus to become the manager of the pupil's learning. This kind of responsibility would require the teacher to have a training which placed at least as much emphasis on pedagogy and on child and adolescent development, as on subject knowledge and understanding.

The inclusive features of the group membership described in the previous paragraph then makes it possible to consider the first requirement mentioned above -- the decoupling of the practical measures for meeting pupils' individual learning needs from the exclusionary associations which they currently engender, and to attempt this within the requirement of economic possibility.

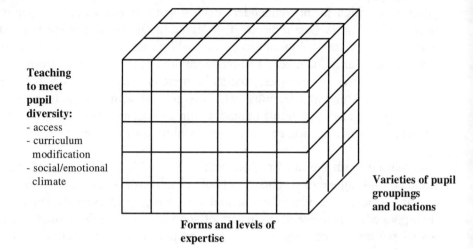

The above figure illustrates three dimensions of an educational approach which is intended to serve this purpose. The analysis is represented in three dimensions in order to make the point that the three aspects of the approach are inextricably linked. Although the analysis is intended to apply to pupil diversity in general, I will refer to the aspects as they concern pupils with special educational needs.

The vertical dimension of particular pedagogical approaches is stated in terms of the three main categories formulated in the Warnock report. "Access" refers particularly to sensory-motor needs. "Modification of the curriculum" represents the approaches to making content accessible conceptually and cognitively. Producing a "social-emotional climate" refers to the measures to meet pupils' emotional and behavioural development within the overall curricular aims. It is therefore particularly related to motivation.

The horizontal dimension refers to the level of pedagogical and other expertise required to support pupils in meeting the various curricular demands. Pupils' progress within a curriculum can be described in terms of the four stages proposed by Haring *et al.* (1978). These refer to Acquisition, fluency, generalisation and adaptation. These in turn, can be considered in relation to the level of pedagogical expertise which is required to support this progress, under the general management of the teacher. *Acquisition* of new learning is likely to require the full expertise of a qualified teacher, who may also need the collaboration or advice from a health or other specialist in the case of pupils with sensory or motor difficulties. Acquisition may also require smaller group teaching. Achieving *fluency* is largely a matter of practice. This clearly can be supported by peer tutoring, parental support, or computer assisted learning. *Generalisation* is likely to be well-mediated by peer group learning or computer assisted learning, or support from teachers' aids, parents and other adults. *Adaptation* may again require closer guidance from the teacher, to consolidate the underlying principles of what is learned, but this can be carried out in collaboration with pupils, parents, and in many instances supported by computer assisted learning. The effectiveness of learning under these arrangements is of course crucially dependent on the monitoring of pupil progress, under the general oversight of the teacher. However, the basic data for this progress monitoring can be generated by all the other agents already mentioned, under the guidance of the teacher.

I have so far referred largely to educational expertise. Pupils who have sensory or motor impairments also need expert support from relevant medical psychological and therapeutic services, and the same applies to pupils with emotional and behaviour difficulties. Increasingly members of these services have realised that they can be far more effective, if they move out of their clinic and hospital bases, and work in collaboration with teachers and parents in schools and the homes of the children concerned. In this way, they can "give away" their skills to teachers, parents and other carers who have the day to day educational responsibility for pupils, and so enhance the support which these can offer. These "experts" have realised that there is then still plenty of demand for their particular professional expertise in both indirect and direct support for pupils.

The third dimension of the matrix refers to grouping and location. The grouping (including individual work) has already be mentioned. The crucial point here is that it is entirely determined by the specific pedagogical demands. Grouping may thus be explicitly planned with cross-achievement membership or according to other principles, such as pupils' behavioural maturity.

Location can become a crucial indicator for pupils that they are being served in an inclusive environment. Studies of the collaboration between mainstream and special schools (NFER, 1992) show how movement of pupils between the schools can go in both directions, and pupils can also learn collaboratively. Such collaboration may in time lead to a merging of location, or a location of a special school within a mainstream school. Learning at the later stages of education is likely to take place in work and other locations within the community, with the involvement of those in those locations.

This brief analysis has only offered an outline of the ideas mentioned. More detailed accounts are available in Wedell (1995). It is important to note that the analysis refers only to practices which already exist. However, it presupposes a high level of pedagogical analysis, and crucially it is predicated on a collaborative ethos among all concerned -- including the pupils. The analysis acknowledges that the current education system is divided into separate elements, but proposes that can to a large degree be overcome by the collaborative approaches of those involved. What is most apparent, perhaps, is that such a system cannot operate on a market-forces competitive basis. At the same time, the emphasis on monitoring pupil progress underlines the paramount importance that the system is tested -- and modified, in relation to the effectiveness of pupils' learning.

The person-power -- and thus the economic implications of the system -- is dealt with by the emphasis on matching expertise to the pedagogical process. This in no way proposes a reduction in teacher-pupil ratios, but it does emphasise the need to capitalise on the person-power available. Crucially, it also involves pupils in taking responsibility for their own learning.

The above analysis has demonstrated the gap between current notions of what is demanded by moves towards integration, and by the development of inclusive policies in education systems. Considered together, these three figures illustrate the question as to how far the education system can be modified to meet the requirements of inclusive education. Hopefully this development will not be held up too long by the current situation in the English education system.

CHAPTER 23

MODELS OF FUNDING TO SUPPORT INCLUSION IN ENGLAND AND WALES

by

Seamus Hegarty

The financing of education in England and Wales is extremely complicated, and the overall picture is not being presented here. One feature of it, however, bears intimately on the financing of special educational provision, namely the wide variability between districts (or local education authorities) in funding levels and allocation practices. This variability is designed to give administrators the flexibility to respond to local needs, in a way that funding by central formula would not permit. In practice, this only works to a partial extent in that there are wide variations in funding levels, as measured by unit expenditure per student, which do not seem to be related to corresponding variations in need.

This of course spills over into funding for special educational provision, since expenditure on students with disabilities or learning difficulties in a district is set within the parameters of general educational expenditure within that district. More importantly for present purposes, this system of funding leads to the emergence of different approaches to allocating resources and indeed to different models of funding.

The traditional approach to funding special educational provision was based on categories of handicap. Special schools were resourced at a certain level depending on the category of students catered for. Thus, schools for the deaf or pupils with severe learning difficulties were funded more generously than schools catering for those with moderate learning difficulties or physical handicaps. So far as formal integration programmes were concerned, the tendency was to set up special classes with a staffing ratio based notionally on a Government circular (4/73), but the lack of coherent resourcing policies on the part of local education authorities and the absence of an established body of practice meant that actual funding levels were determined very much by local factors, particularly the persuasiveness of the school principal and his/her skill in working the system !

Funding for students with less pronounced -- but still significant -- difficulties was ad hoc in the extreme. There was a large group of students -- famously estimated in the Warnock Report (Department of Education and Science, 1978) to number 20 per cent of the school population -- who were not formally identified as handicapped but were failing in school none the less and had clear need of additional support. Whether or not particular schools were resourced to provide this extra support depended largely on individual initiative and opportunity, and students' receipt of such a support owed much to happenstance.

Major changes in special education were introduced with the Education Act 1981 (implemented in 1983). These changes were not concerned primarily with resourcing -- it was nearly a decade later before structural changes in school funding were made -- but they radically altered the way in which students with difficulties in school were regarded and the context within which educational provision was made for them. Categories of handicap were abandoned and the concept of "special educational needs" was given legislative definition. The Act introduced Statements of Special Educational Needs, making an explicit record of a student's special educational needs and how in detail they were to be met. This brought a new element into the funding system in that for some students resourcing was tied to the individual.

The 1981 Act was widely criticised as a "no-resources" measure: schools and local education authorities were being given many new responsibilities but without receiving any extra resources. In the event, numerous positive developments took place and the Act turned out to be a potent lever for action. These included more systematic assessment, more explicit links between assessment outcomes and provision, increased participation by parents and of course a gradual shift in the conceptual map of special education away from child-centred notions of defect to the interactive concept of special educational needs and the imperatives of whole-school reform. Specifically on the resources front, the Act led to local education authorities devoting a greater proportion of their budgets to special needs provision (Goacher et al., 1988). This was partly to underpin assessment and statementing activity but it also resulted in expanded support services (Gipps, Gross and Goldstein, 1987). One study identified a shift in the modus operandi of support services which favoured inclusive education, for example by switching the focus of their work in schools from individual students to teachers and helping to build up the latter's competence in including all students within a common curriculum framework (Moses, Hegarty and Jowett, 1988).

The funding of schools, including special educational provision, underwent major changes in the wake of the 1988 Education Act and subsequent Government circulars. The key element has been the transfer of budgets and spending decisions to schools. Every local education authority has had to construct a formula for calculating school budgets, including staffing costs, and hand over control of the budget to school governing bodies.

This has led to major changes in the educational system -- and not just fiscal changes. Indeed, the devolution of responsibility and the corresponding increase in local autonomy entailed in this reform are a central plank in the Government's efforts to improve student achievement.

Funding by formula has had particular impact on special educational provision. Officers in local education authorities were accustomed to exercising discretion in allocating extra resources to schools where they felt the need was greatest -- or whose principals were most persistent. Special discretion is no longer possible: schools have to be funded on a common basis, and any extra resources must be allocated by a specific, public formula.

In outline, schools' basic funding contains a notional element for special educational provision, and they can receive additional funding geared to special needs in a number of ways. The main part of the budget is allocated, in a common way for all schools in a district, by reference to pupil numbers and their ages with some allowance for factors such as size of school. The notional element for special educational provision is to cover those things that every school is deemed to be doing in terms of additional teaching time, in-class support and so on. The precise amount included under this heading is not spelt out, and there is no direct monitoring of the school's provision in relation to it.

The first way in which schools can receive extra resources relates to pupils with less serious special educational needs. This is most often based on a simple formula based for example on take up of free school meals, reading test scores or national curriculum assessment results. This is based on the assumption that socio-economic disadvantage is correlated with incidence of pupils with learning difficulties, so when a school has a higher than average level of social disadvantage it can be expected to have a higher than average number of pupils needing additional support. If this assumption is valid, a measure of socio-economic disadvantage can be used as a proxy of the incidence of special educational needs and additional resources allocated accordingly.

The most commonly used proxy measure is the number of free school meals taken in a school: English schools provide a midday meal which children pay for, but if they cannot easily pay there are procedures by which they are given a meal free of charge. This procedure has the advantage of being administratively simple -- eligibility for free school meals is determined separately, and the information is available for use. There is, moreover, a good deal of evidence linking socio-economic disadvantage and learning difficulties. There are of course difficulties with the approach. Apart from the obvious crudeness of using proxy measures, there are weaknesses in the free school meals indicator -- children do not have to take the school meal and some choose not to, some families who are eligible for free school meals do not have them, and in some areas cultural attitudes impinge on the take up of free school meals as much as the level of disadvantage. All of these affect the link between free school meals and special educational needs and call into question the efficacy of using the former as a measure of the latter.

A second way in which schools can receive extra funds relates to pupils with more marked difficulties. These pupils will often be the subject of a formal Statement of Special Educational Needs, and their needs are resource-intensive. How exactly to allocate resources in these cases is the subject of much debate and experimentation, and practice varies widely. Increasingly, these decisions are based on an authority-wide audit so that all pupils who require additional help are treated in a common way.

In one authority (Avon), the audit is based on a Special Provision Matrix, which has to be completed for each pupil deemed to require extra help. The potential help is broken down into eight areas or dimensions: the academic curriculum; the social curriculum; special resources (equipment and materials); therapy; physical requirements; assessment and review; type and level of adult contacts; situation and transport. In addition, the help can be presented at any one of six levels ranging from arrangements schools can put into place from their own resources to resource-intensive programmes that require external support.

This profile is completed for each pupil on the basis of a multi-disciplinary assessment and so will reflect advice and perspectives from teachers, parents, relevant professionals and local authority officers. As such, it should be based upon a clear description of the pupil's learning and/or behaviour difficulties, accounts of the provision required in different areas and a clear statement of short- and long-term objectives for the pupil. When completed the profile is translated into units of funding, and the school receives a sum of money based on the number of units and their value. The value of the unit funding can vary, in respect of inflation, local authority policy *and* total number of units of funding being sought. Broadly speaking, the total quantum of expenditure in a district is fixed and, if in a given year the number of units of funding sought is very high, the value of the unit will necessarily be reduced.

Other auditing arrangements follow this general approach, though not necessarily using such a detailed matrix of provision. A feature of interest in some districts is the use of a representative panel to moderate the bids made by schools and effectively decide on resource allocation. These panels tend to include school principals, special needs co-ordinators and representatives of the learning support and psychology services. Another growing feature is the requirement on schools when making a bid to specify what they are doing to meet that pupil's needs at the moment.

A third way of allocating extra resources to schools focuses specifically on **projects** designed to promote inclusion. This approach switches the emphasis from individual students to school-wide initiatives which enhance the school's ability to educate students with special educational needs, and targets resources accordingly.

An example from Nottinghamshire will illustrate the approach. In this district schools are grouped on an area basis, and all additional resources for special educational needs are channelled through Mainstream Support Groups. These consist of local authority officers, representatives of the advisory and support services, school psychologists and school principals.

Each group has a fixed sum of money for disbursement to schools. The first call on this money is still students who place exceptional demands on schools, but a sizeable amount is available for inclusion projects. Proposals are sought from schools, either individually or in consortium with one or more partner schools, "to establish provision in order to increase their ability to provide for their own children with special needs as an alternative to special school placements". Project funds cover additional staff and resources as well as increased access to external support services. Project funds normally last for one to two years and are monitored by the Mainstream Support Group.

Also covered within this source of funding are projects designed to assist special schools in becoming an area support base for neighbourhood schools. While the thrust of the various initiatives is to reduce special school numbers, special schools are valued as a reservoir of expertise. Attempts are being made to capitalise on that expertise by reshaping the mission of the special school and making the necessary financial changes to underline and facilitate the new mission.

Conclusion

I want to conclude by picking out some of the more interesting aspects of emerging practice. These are not present everywhere but they are sufficiently common to merit noting.

- Additional resources are being provided to schools in a common, explicit way with criteria and procedures visible for all to see.

- There is a focus on evidence, both by way of requiring schools to say what they are doing with pupils already and what they propose to do with any additional resources.

- There is a greater involvement of the schools in deciding how district funds should be provided to individual schools -- this involvement and the explicit nature of the decision-making help to reduce undue competitiveness between schools.

- Monitoring of the way in which extra resources are spent is taken for granted.

- New roles are being sought for special schools that bring them within the framework of other schools in the neighbourhood and enable them to support inclusive education, and these new roles are being supported by appropriate financial arrangements.

- There is a switch from providing extra funds for individual pupils to supporting projects which enhance the school's capacity to deal more effectively with a wide range of pupils, in effect to target funds explicitly on promoting inclusive education.

CHAPTER 24

FISCAL ISSUES RELATED TO THE INCLUSION OF STUDENTS WITH DISABILITIES IN SCHOOLS IN THE UNITED STATES

by

Thomas B. Parrish

Introduction

This paper examines the relationship between fiscal policies in special education and the requirement under federal law in the United States that students with disabilities be educated in the least restrictive environment (LRE) appropriate to their needs.[1] Meeting the LRE requirement is complicated by the sometimes competing requirement under the federal Individuals with Disabilities Education Act (IDEA) that a "continuum of services" be made available for students with disabilities. The essence of this requirement is that an array of alternative placement options must be made available for special education students to assure that appropriate choices are available. While some policymakers use the LRE requirement to argue that more restrictive placement options (*e.g.*, special schools) are no longer needed, others point to the "continuum of services" provision to counter that they are not only needed, but required.

This paper does not attempt to resolve the tension that appears between these two provisions, but discusses the relationship between fiscal policies in special education and the program goals policymakers set for these programs. For example, although the continuum of services requirement does not suggest that there should be fiscal incentives *favouring* more restrictive placements, it is argued that such fiscal incentives should be identified and removed since they clearly conflict with the IDEA of the LRE requirements. Whether the resulting fiscal policies should simply be free of any placement incentives, or should actually *favour* less restrictive placements is a matter for local, state, and federal policymakers to determine. However, it will be argued that in considering alternative fiscal policies, a conscious effort *must* be made to consider the placement incentives associated with each alternative and to develop future fiscal provisions with their relationship to the state's program goals clearly in mind.

The provision of special education services in the United States[2]

Prior to World War II, children and youth with disabilities were generally denied the right to a public education in the United States, although separate schools or institutions for children with particular disabilities (such as deafness and blindness) were established as early as the 1820s in some

---

1. The concept of least restrictive environment (LRE) is sometimes operationally defined by the terms "inclusion" or "integration" of students with disabilities into general education schools and classrooms.
2. This section borrows heavily from Verstegen (1994).

states. State compulsory attendance laws, which began to be passed in the late nineteenth century, also generally allowed for the exclusion of exceptional children who could not "profit from an education." In other states, provisions allowed children with disabilities to be excluded from publicly supported education if no "appropriate" program was available or if special transportation was required. Slowly throughout the twentieth century, several states upgraded their special education programs and services; however, they were relatively few in number until given impetus by the post-war civil rights movement, when the parents of exceptional students began to organise and demand educational services "not as a matter of charity, but as a civil right." (Mosher, Hastings, and Wagoner, 1979, pp. 16 *ff.*)

Subsequently, in 1975, extensive hearings to extend and amend the Education of the Handicapped Amendments of 1974 were held by the House Subcommittee on Select Education and the Senate Subcommittee on the Handicapped. Testimony indicated that a large percentage of children with disabilities remained unserved or underserved across the states, often due to state financial constraints. For example, statistics provided by the Bureau of Education for the Handicapped estimated that of the more than eight million children (birth through 21 years) with disabilities requiring special education and related services, only half (3.9 million) were receiving an appropriate education; 1.75 million children with disabilities, "usually those with the most severe disabilities," were receiving no education at all; and 2.5 million children with disabilities were receiving an inappropriate education (US Senate, 1976, pp. 131, 198).

The resulting federal legislation, later renamed as the IDEA, authorised federal aid to the states of up to 40 per cent of the average per pupil expenditure (APPE) across the nation if the states would elect to participate in this national program. It guaranteed a "free and appropriate public education" to all students with disabilities, with the exact provisions of each student's program to be designed according to specifications prescribed for each child in an "individualised education program". Although all states eventually elected to participate in this federal initiative, in fact, the federal share of funding has never come close to meeting the expected level of support. Consequently, the federal government is by far the junior partner in the provision of special education services across the US, providing only an estimated 8 per cent of special education funds. The remainder of special education funding comes from state and local sources, with the relative percentages varying considerably by state. However, despite its relatively low level of financial aid, federal policy through the IDEA and other federal statutes, such as the Americans with Disabilities Act (ADA) continue to exert considerable influence on special education policy across the nation.

Increasing the degree of participation of students with disabilities in general education programs is a goal that is commonly held at the federal level and across the states. Although these policies have recently received new emphasis with the widespread interest in issues related to special education inclusion, in fact they are clearly found in the initial LRE provisions of the IDEA. However, it is becoming increasingly clear that special education fiscal policies sometimes affect program provision in unanticipated ways and may now sometimes serve as a barrier to the implementation of more integrated and inclusive programming for students with disabilities. Governmental statements of support for more inclusive placements are not likely to change local practice if the accompanying fiscal provisions actively discourage them.

The effects of fiscal policy on program provision

Each of the states and the federal government has a different set of policies and procedures for determining allocations of special education aid to local school districts. Each has been designed to achieve different policy and program objectives. Some tend to be more supportive of inclusive placements and integrated services than others. However, the purpose of this paper is not to endorse any single funding approach, but to present a set of general principles. These are *a)* that financing policy *will* influence local program provision; *b)* that there are *no* incentive-free financing systems; and consequently *c)* that in developing fiscal policy, it is essential to develop provisions that will *support*, or at least *not obstruct*, program goals. *In short, prior to the design of funding provisions, it is imperative to determine specific goals for a given social intervention and then to design the financing system accordingly.*[3]

Thus, prior to considering the relationship between special education finance policies and the removal of incentives for restrictive placements, it is necessary to develop some agreed upon definition of the specific reforms being pursued. Such reforms generally include the removal of fiscal incentives for placing students in private over public schools, in specialised over neighbourhood schools, and in segregated classrooms and settings throughout the school day. However, they may also include issues related to greater flexibility in the use of local resources, the creation of an intervention systems for *all* students, and the creation of fiscal disincentives for labelling students as "special education."

These issues are pertinent for several reasons. First, one way to avoid restrictiveness in the placement of students is to avoid fiscal incentives for identifying students as special education in the first place *when alternative types of interventions may be sufficient to meet their needs.* For example, the removal of fiscal incentives to identify more special education students is a stated policy objective of recently enacted special education finance reforms in the states of South Dakota, Vermont, Pennsylvania, Massachusetts and Montana. This is also an element contained in the recent recommendation issued by the US Department of Education related to federal funding allocations under the IDEA. Removing incentives to overidentify special education students is also an incentive because of the continuing rise in special education enrolments issue in the United States. Approximately 10 percent of all school aged children are identified as eligible for special education in the United States, with the number of students receiving such services rising by 4.2 per cent between the 1992-93 and 1993-94 school years. This represents the largest one year increase since national tracking of these data began in 1976.

A related objective for program reform is to provide a seamless set of services to meet the needs of *all* students -- whether they have general, special, bilingual, poverty-related or "compensatory" education requirements. This strategy attempts to reduce the barriers built around these categorical programs, which result in the separation of associated programs and services. These barriers lead to the inefficient use of resources through the required maintenance of multiple administrative units, accounting structures, and facilities; and to the inefficient provision of services for students with multiple special needs. The separation of these services may also be seen as leading to more restrictive service models.[4]

The concept that appropriate instructional programs and related services cannot be provided without adequate financial support has long been recognised. However, a newer concept that is becoming widely recognised is that the *policies* that underlie educational financing mechanisms may be as important in affecting program provision as the *amounts* allocated. Even the simplest funding

---

3.   For a more thorough discussion of these issues, see Parrish (1994).

4.   For a discussion of these issues at the local and federal levels in the United States, see McLaughlin (1995) and Verstegen (1995).

systems contain incentives and disincentives that directly influence the orientation, quantities, and types of services to be provided at the local level.

State fiscal policies affecting the placement of students with disabilities

Special education finance reform is currently being actively considered in approximately two-thirds of the 50 states in the US. Telephone interviews with state directors of special education or their representatives indicate that the desire for flexibility in the use of special education resources and the need to remove fiscal incentives favouring more restrictive placements are among the major factors providing impetus for change. In states where fiscal incentives for utilising segregated programs are a major issue, two principal, and often separate, elements of the funding provisions are motivating reform. These elements are *a)* aid differentials within the public system that relate to type of placement, and *b)* differentials between the amounts of state aid received for services provided in local schools as opposed to comparable services provided in more remote centralised private or public special education settings.

States with public funding differentials favouring placements in separate classrooms, schools, or facilities tend to be those in which the amount of funding received varies based on the primary setting in which students receive services. These types of funding systems generally feature an array of primary service configurations, with state aid varying by type of placement. The concept underlying this type of system is that the amount of aid a district receives for a student with special needs should be directly related to the cost of providing services for the student. Since all categorical funding formulas have an underlying cost rationale, many school finance experts and policymakers have preferred systems that differentiate funding amounts on actual differences in the cost of services. Although this reasoning is clearly sound, such cost-based systems are problematic when they create clear fiscal incentives for higher cost placements provided in separate classrooms or facilities.

A second practice that relates to funding incentives for restrictive placements is the use of separate special education funding mechanisms for public and private special education schools. Issues relating to fiscal incentives for private placements seem especially difficult for states to resolve. For example, although Massachusetts recently made major changes in its public special education funding system, incentives for public schools to use private placements were retained. Similar concerns have been raised in New York, where a proposal to remove incentives to use private placements has met considerable resistance. Use of private placements varies considerably across the states. While states like New York and New Jersey show 7 and 5.75 per cent of their special education students in private placements, respectively, Wisconsin shows less than .05 per cent and Utah, 0 per cent.

Centralised public schools (*e.g.*, a state school for the blind) for selected populations of students with low incidence special needs can also create public policy dilemmas. It is not that the existence of such schools is problematic. In fact, they clearly seem to fall within the IDEA requirement that a "continuum of services" be available to students with special needs. However, state special education funding provisions conflict with the LRE requirement of the IDEA when they clearly *favour* those types of centralised placements *over* the provision of services in local districts. The state of Missouri serves as a case in point. Students with mental retardation may be served in state schools, which maintain a source of state support that is entirely separate from the state's special education funding system, at a cost of about $15 000 per student. Alternately, local districts may opt to serve them despite the fact that virtually no supplemental state aid is available for this type of local service. As parents are increasingly demanding the provision of local, fully integrated services, school district officials are becoming increasingly disgruntled over the lack of state financial support for those type of services. State officials are caught in a dilemma because, while they wish to promote local provision in less restrictive settings, they are well aware that the state's current fiscal policies clearly serve as a deterrent to this kind of change.

What seems important from a fiscal policy perspective is that state funding systems should *not favour private or separate public placements.* Funding for high cost students should *follow* students to local school districts, where decisions are best made about whether these dollars should be invested in contracted or locally provided services.

Another important issue relating to local flexibility in the use of funds as districts incorporate less restrictive placement patterns relates to separate, categorical funding for transportation services. As districts attempt to move students with disabilities back to their neighbourhood schools, they face start-up costs in relation to making these schools fully accessible and in purchasing multiple sets of specialised equipment, rather than just the one set that may be needed in a single specialised school. These costs may be largely offset through savings in transportation costs. However, in state funding systems where transportation is categorically funded, dollars saved through reduced transportation services cannot be recouped for use in other ways (*i.e.*, to support the start-up costs of more integrated programs in neighbourhood schools).

Conclusion

Clearly, fiscal policy has the capacity to drive or deter reform. However, it is also clear that changes in fiscal policy alone are unlikely to be sufficient to cause program change. States reporting the most success in co-ordinating program and fiscal reform emphasise the need for financial incentives, or at least the removal of disincentives, as well as the provision of a comprehensive system of professional development and ongoing support to effect such desired program changes as the implementation of fully integrated education services for all students.

CHAPTER 25

STANDARDS AND ASSESSMENT IN THE UNITED STATES INCLUDING STUDENTS WITH DISABILITIES IN PUBLIC ACCOUNTABILITY SYSTEMS

by

Martha L. Thurlow[5]

Introduction

In 1990, the United States Office of Special Education Programs first funded the National Center on Educational Outcomes (NCEO). Its original purpose was to work with state and federal agencies to identify a conceptual model of the important outcomes of education for students with disabilities, and to look at what we know about the current educational outcomes of these students.

In order to examine the outcomes of education, NCEO staff had to obtain information from existing public education accountability systems. In the strictest sense, an educational accountability system is one that includes goals, indicators of success toward meeting those goals, analyses of data, reporting procedures, and a set of consequences. In the United States, there are both national data collection systems and state data collection systems. Similarly, there are goals being set at the national level and in many of the 50 states in the US. Even at the local school district level, within states, educational goals are being set.

The numerous goals that exist, and that are being developed, are too many to describe. Yet, there are certain themes that are evident regardless of the level of the goals -- local, state, or federal. First, the goals usually are said to be for "all" students, even though the individuals who developed the goals may not have considered students in special education when they developed the goals. Second, academic achievement is emphasised, even though other kinds of goals exist. Third, these goals may be described as standards, but most focus on content to be learned rather than performance levels to be attained. Fourth, educators are struggling with the issue of whether there should be the same standards for all students, or whether a separate set or a modified set of standards should apply to students with disabilities.

At the same time that all this is happening, there is also a tremendous push to assess the educational attainment of students. Even when standards have not been defined, the academic performance of students in core academic areas is being assessed in an attempt to keep public education accountable for results.

---

5. The preparation of this paper was supported, in part, through a co-operative agreement (H159600004), between the U.S. Department of Education, Office of Special Education Programs, and the university of Minnesota. Opinions do not necessarily represent those of the US Department of Education or Offices within it.

Educational accountability systems in the United States

The primary national assessment used to check the educational performance of students in the United States is the National Assessment of Educational Progress (NAEP). Every two years or less, students in grades 4, 8, and 12 are assessed in one or more content areas. The content areas vary from one year to another, and are administered to samples of students across the United States.

Over time, NAEP has been transformed into an accountability tool in the USA This is occurring, in part, because standards of performance are being applied to scores (from basic, to proficient, to advanced), and in part because of the addition of a state-level version of NAEP. The state-level assessment is being used on a trial basis, and therefore is known as NAEP-Trial State Assessment (TSA). When performance on NAEP-TSA is reported, states are typically listed in order according to the scores. Those at the top are the ones whose students are performing best on NAEP. The listing of states is presented in newspapers across the nation and in national news magazines. Public reporting of performance thus has become a consequence of importance to states.

Many states in the USA also have their own assessment and accountability systems. In some of these, performance is reported at the school district and school levels, like NAEP-TSA is reported for states. In 1995, 43 of the 50 states in the USA were using a state assessment to measure the performance of students. Of the seven not using state assessments, three were not doing so because they were in the process of revising their assessments, and two others were in the process of developing state assessments for future use. Thus, it is evident that assessment and accountability systems are an important part of the state educational system as well as the national system.

In the USA, there are also many local school district and school assessments that are used for accountability purposes. These contribute to the millions of tests administered each day in the USA, as reported by the Office of Technology Assessment (1992) in *Testing in American Schools*. These assessments, however, are not the focus of discussion here. Rather, the focus is on state and federal public accountability systems in the USA, and the inclusion of students with disabilities in these systems.

What we know about students with disabilities in the United States accountability systems

There is much support for the general conclusion that too many students with disabilities have been excluded from educational accountability systems in the United States. The support comes from studies conducted by NCEO (McGrew, Thurlow, Shriner and Spiegel, 1992; McGrew, Thurlow and Spiegel, 1993), by the National Center for Education Statistics (Houser, 1995), and by the National Academy of Education (1992).

For the national-level NAEP, it was first estimated that approximately 50 per cent of all students with disabilities were excluded (McGrew *et al.*, 1993). This estimate was later increased as a result of a study by the agency contracting for the administration of NAEP (Houser, 1995). That study revealed that 66 per cent of students with disabilities had been excluded in the 1992 administration of NAEP.

At the state level, it was found that exclusion rates vary tremendously from one state to another. Specifically, in 1990, the range of exclusion was from 33 per cent in one state to 87 per cent in another state. Such variations do not reflect variations in the identification of students with disabilities (see US Department of Education, 1994). The variations are troubling also because all states were to use the same exclusion criteria when making decisions about whether students should be excluded from taking the assessment.

Additional evidence of the over-exclusion issue comes from states' own assessments. Directors of special education, and assessment personnel in states, have indicated exclusion rates that vary from 0 per cent to 100 per cent of students with disabilities in their state assessments. This means that in at least one state, none of the students with disabilities (regardless of type of disability) participates in the state assessment, while in at least one other state, all of the students with disabilities participate in the state assessment or accountability system.

Consequences of exclusion from public accountability systems

Exclusion from public accountability systems can have very significant consequences for students in the US. First, when students with disabilities are not included in the pool of information upon which educational reform decisions are made, they are not considered when reforms are devised and they do not have an impact on those reforms.

Second, when students with disabilities are not included in public accountability systems, we get an inaccurate picture of the status of education. This becomes especially important as schools in the US move toward more inclusive instructional systems. However, regardless of the extent to which an instructional system is inclusive, it is important for the public accountability systems to be completely inclusive. This is the only way to avoid unintended consequences of exclusion.

At present we know only a little about some of the unintended consequences of exclusion. One of these has been identified by Richard Allington and Anne McGill-Franzen (1992). They found an increase in referrals to special education when schools were allowed to exempt students in special education from assessments used to determine which schools received rewards for good performance. If all students had unequivocally been included in the accountability system, referrals of students to special education would not have increased when tests were to be administered.

The issue of exclusion of some or all students receiving special education services is also a significant issue for international comparisons. Unfortunately, we still know very little about the rates of participation of students with disabilities in international assessments, much less in assessments within countries (Elliott *et al.,* 1995).

When exclusion occurs

The three most common points in the assessment process at which exclusion of students with disabilities occurs are at the time of test development, during the administration of an assessment, and in the reporting of results (Ysseldyke, Thurlow, McGrew and Shriner, 1994; Ysseldyke, Thurlow, McGrew and Vanderwood, 1994).

During test development. The most common way in which exclusion occurs is to not consider students with disabilities when an assessment is being constructed. Often this means that an appropriate lower extension of the test is not produced. But beyond this, it also often means that when a test is standardised, students with disabilities are not included in the standardisation process. When these kinds of exclusions have occurred at the development phase, it is almost impossible to include students with disabilities during the administration of the test. This requires that other types of accountability measures be used to include students with disabilities. This approach is taken in some states in the US. For example, in one state students with disabilities are not included in the state assessment, but are included in the accountability system by factoring in measures of attendance and dropping out of school.

During administration. Exclusion of students with disabilities during the administration of an assessment is the kind of exclusion usually thought of first. This happens when states have assessment policies that suggest that students with disabilities do not need to take an assessment if they are not in the mainstream classroom for at least a certain percentage of time (usually 50 per cent), if they might be emotionally upset by the process, or if someone decides they do not want them to take the test. The vagueness of such guidelines, unfortunately, has resulted in highly variable exclusion practices from one place to the next. Furthermore, it opens the door to inappropriate practices, such as scheduling field trips for special education students on days when assessments are to be administered, a single person (such as a school principal) deciding who will not take an assessment in a school, or the decision about participation being made after the assessment has been administered (as in an interpretation that the results of an administered assessment do not reflect what a student really knows and, therefore, the student should not have taken the test, and it will be discarded). These are all occurrences that have been documented in one way or another to have occurred as a result of having public accountability systems that do not require the participation of all students.

In reporting. When assessment results are reported, there is also great potential for over-exclusion of students with disabilities. States in the US vary tremendously in how they report assessment results (Thurlow, Scott and Ysseldyke, 1995). Some guidelines explicitly indicate that when students with disabilities take an assessment, their scores are not to be included when the results are published. In some states, this type of exclusion only occurs in certain situations (such as when the student's instruction in the area being assessed is provided through special education services).

How can all students be included in public accountability systems?

In general, there are three ways in which students with disabilities can participate in public accountability systems: *1)* in the standard way, without accommodations, *2)* with accommodations in assessment, and *3)* by using different procedures. Estimated percentages of students with disabilities requiring these different approaches are shown in the following diagram. These percentages were estimated on the basis of the percentages of students with disabilities of varying degrees of severity in the United States (Ysseldyke, Thurlow, McGrew and Shriner, 1994). Although they are guesses, these estimates are supported by recent follow-up studies of students with disabilities who were excluded from the 1994 NAEP-TSA (National Academy of Education, in press).

Perhaps the first step is for public accountability systems to be public about their rates of exclusion. It is important to report both the number included and the number excluded, and to be very clear about what is in the denominator when percentages are provided. We have found that different states have different views of what the number is that represents the total possible (Erickson, Thurlow and Ysseldyke, 1995). For example, some states exclude students in separate schools, while others do not count students in ungraded programs. It will be very important to confirm that "all" means "all" and that this applies to all students with disabilities, regardless of whether they are in the general educational system.

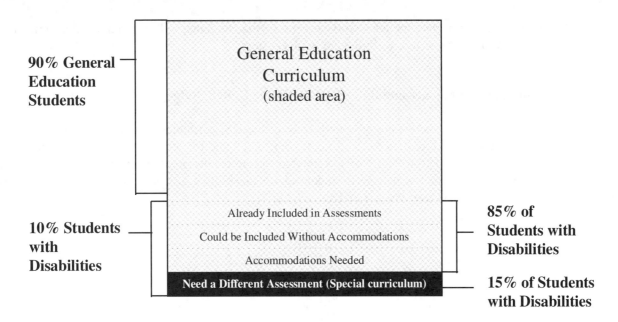

In the United States, one state (Kentucky) currently has a public accountability system that is perhaps as close as possible to the desired "full-participation" system. The basic tenets of this system are that "all children can learn" and that "schools are accountable for all students". With these as the foundation, it is a logical extension that all children should be in the public educational accountability system. The state started out by defining a common set of six goals for all students in its educational system. They are that all students will be able to:

- use basic communication and math skills for purposes and situations they encounter in life;
- apply core concepts and principles from mathematics, the sciences, arts and humanities, social studies, practical living studies and vocational studies for purposes and situations they encounter in life;
- become self-sufficient individuals;
- become responsible members of a family, work group, or community;
- think and solve problems across the variety of situations they encounter in life; and,
- connect and integrate the knowledge they have gained in school into their own lives.

From these goals, 75 valued learner expectancies were defined. Then open-ended items and performance events were constructed to assess performance on the expectancies. For the students with more significant cognitive disabilities, a subset of these learner expectancies was identified as most relevant to their educational programs, and thus the focus of their assessments. For all other students, performance was obtained either in the standard way (through open ended and performance assessments, and via portfolios), or with the use of accommodations and adaptations in the assessment process. For those students with the most severe cognitive disabilities, an alternate portfolio system was used.

Regardless of the exact assessment approach used, all students count equally in the state's public accountability system. In addition, students' scores are applied to their home schools, regardless of their current location of service delivery. The application of scores in this way has actually encouraged the return of some students in residential placements back to their home schools, where those who receive the students' scores can be directly responsible for the education that determines what scores the students attain. All of these factors together have resulted in a public educational accountability system that includes 100 per cent of its students. The potential for unintended consequences should be virtually eliminated in this system.

The future of education accountability systems in the United States

Many changes in practice are now underway in the US, particularly in regard to accountability systems in education. More than ever before, there is a demand for schools and school systems (state and federal levels included) to be more accountable for the results of education for all students. This aim will be furthered, and will benefit students with disabilities, to the extent that truly inclusive public accountability systems emerge and are valued.

REFERENCES

AINSCOW, M. (1991), "Towards Effective Schools for All: Some Problems and Possibilities", in Ainscow, M. (ed.), *Effective Schools for All, op.cit.,* pp. 215-228.

AINSCOW, M. (1995), "Education for All: Making it Happen", *Support for Learning*, 10 (4), pp. 147-157.

ALLINGTON, R.L. and MCGILL-FRANZEN, A (1992), "Intended Effects of Educational Reform in New York", *Educational Policy*, 6 (4), pp. 397-414.

ANDERSON, G.M., and NELSON, N.W. (1988), "Integrating language intervention and education in an alternate adolescent language program", Seminars in Speech and Language, 9, pp. 341-353.

ANDERSSON, Y. (1978), "Family interaction and personality development", International Symposium: Speech and Development of the Personality of the Deaf, Federation of the Deaf and the Hard of Hearing in the German Democratic Republic, Leipzig.

APPELHANS, P. (1993), "Integration of Visually Impaired Students", *European Journal of Special Needs Education*, 8, 3, pp. 221-239.

ARMSTRONG, T. (1994), *Multiple Intelligences in the Classroom*, Association for Supervision and Curriculum Development, Alexandria, Va.

ASSOCIATION OF ICELANDIC SPECIAL TEACHERS (1994), *Special Education: The Role And Domain of Special Teachers*, Reykjavik.

ASTUTO, T.A., CLARK, D.L., READ, A., McGREE, K. AND deKOVEN PELTON FERNANDEZ, L. (1994), "Roots of Reform: Challenging the Assumptions that Control Change in Education", *Phi Delta Kappan*, Educational Foundation, Bloomington, In.

BALLANTI, G. and FONTANA, L. (1989), *Discorso E Azione Nella Pedagogia Scientifica: Analisi E Programmazione Per Un'educazione Individualizzata*, 4th ed. (1st ed. 1981), Lisciani & Giunti, Teramo, Italy.

BERNDT, J. and FALCONER, A. (1991), "Physical Therapy in the Educational Setting", in Campbell, S. (ed.), *Pediatric Neurologic Physical Therapy* (2nd ed.), Churchill-Livingstone, New York, pp. 261-296.

BLESS, G. (1995), *Zur Wirksamkeit der Integration. Forschungsüberblick, praktische Umsetzung einer integrativen Schulform, Untersuchungen zum Lernfortschritt*, Bern Stuttgart Wien (Haupt).

BRADLEY, L. and BRYANT, P. (1985), *Rhyme and Reason in Reading and Spelling,* University of Michigan Press, Ann Arbor.

BROOKS, J.G. and BROOKS, M. (1993), *In Search of Understanding: The Case for Constructivist Classrooms*, ASCD, Alexandria, Va.

BRYJAK, G.J. and SOROKA, M.P (1994), *Sociology: Cultural Diversity in a Changing World,* 2nd ed., Allyn and Bacon, Boston.

BUNDESAMT FÜR STATISTIK (BFS) (1994), *Schülerinnen, Schüler und Studierende 1993/94 -- Elèves et étudiants 1993/94",* Bern.

CAMPBELL, C., CAMPBELL, S., COLLICOTT, J., PERNER, D. and STONE, J. (1988), "Adapting regular class curriculum for integrated special needs students", *Education New Brunswick Journal*, 3, pp. 17-20.

CAMPBELL, P.H., MCINERNEY, W.F., and COOPER, M.A. (1984), "Therapeutic programming for students with severe handicaps", *American Journal of Occupational Therapy*, 38, pp. 594-599.

CANEVARO, A. (1987), *Handicap E Scuola: Manuale Per L'integrazione Scolastica*, NIS, Rome.

CARNEVALE, A.D., GAINER, L.J. and MELTZER, A.S. (1990), *Workplace Basics: The Skills Employers Want,* Jossey-Bass, San Francisco.

CCE (1994), "The quality of education", *The Magazine*, No. 2, pp. 14-15, European Commission Task Force on Human Resources, Education, Training and Youth, Brussels.

CENTRAAL BUREAU VOOR DE STATISTIEK (1993), *Statistiek van het basisonderwijs, het speciaal onderwijs en het voortgezet speciaal onderwijs 1992/'93*, Scholen en leerlingen, 's-Gravenhage, SDU.

CHALFANT, J., PYSH, M. and MOULTRIE, R. (1979), "Teacher assistant teams: a model for within-building problem solving", *Learning Disabilities Quarterly*, 2(3), pp. 85-96.

COLLICOTT, J. (1991), "Implementing Multi-Level Instruction: Strategies for Classroom Teachers", in Porter, G.L. and Richter, D. (eds.), *Changing Canadian Schools,* The Roeher Institute, North York, Ontario, pp. 191-218.

COLLICOTT, J. and PORTER, G.L. (1992), "New Brunswick School Districts 28 and 29: Mandates and Strategies that Promote Inclusive Schooling", in Villa, R., Thousand, J., Stainback, S., and Stainback, W. (eds.), *Restructuring for Caring and Effective Education: an Administrative Guide to Creating Heterogeneous Schools*, Paul Brookes Publishing, Baltimore.

COMMISSION OF THE EUROPEAN COMMUNITIES (1988), "Social Europe", Report on the fight against illiteracy, Supplement 2/88, Office for Official Publications of the European Communities, Luxembourg.

CONLEY, D.T. (1993), *Roadmap to Restructuring: Policies, Practices and the Emerging Visions of Schooling*, ERIC Clearing House on Educational Management, University of Oregon, Eugene, Or.

COUTINHO, M. (1991), "How the past affects the present: Meeting students' needs in tomorrow's schools", *AOTA Self Study Series: School-based practice for related services*, AOTA, Rockville, Maryland.

CRAWFORD, C. and PORTER, G.L. (1992), *How it Happens: a Look at Inclusive Educational Practice in Canada for Children and Youth with Disabilities*, The Roeher Institute, North York, Ontario.

CUBAN, L. (1984), *How Teachers Taught: Constancy and Change in American Classrooms, 1890-1980*, Longman, New York.

DARLING-HAMMOND, L. (1993), "Reforming the School Reform Agenda: Developing Capacity for School Transformation", *Phi Delta Kappan*, June, pp. 753-761.

DE ANNA, L. (1992), *Integrazione Scolastica. Francia E Italia: Modelli Operativi E Sistemi A Confronto*, L'ed., Rome.

DE ANNA, L. (1992), "Report of the italian delegation on Phase I of the OECD Project on Active Life for Handicapped Adolescents: School Integration", mimeo, available from author.

DE ANNA, L. (1993), "Report of the Italian delegation on Phase II of the OECD Project on Active Life for Handicapped Adolescents: School Integration", mimeo, available from author.

DENO, E. (1970), "Special Education as Developmental", *Exceptional Children*, 37, pp. 229-237.

DENS, A. *et al.* (1994), "The Role of Support Services in the Development of 'Inclusive Education': a European Reflection on a New Profile for the Psycho-Medical-Social Centres in Flanders", Helios Seminar, PMS Centre for Special Education, Leuven.

DEPARTMENT FOR EDUCATION (1992), "Exclusions", discussion paper, DFE, London.

DEPARTMENT FOR EDUCATION (1993), *Education Act 1993*, HMSO, London.

DEPARTMENT FOR EDUCATION (1994), *The Code of Practice on the Identification and Assessment of Special Educational Needs*, DFE, London.

DEPARTMENT OF EDUCATION AND SCIENCE (1978), "Special educational needs", the Warnock Report, DES, London.

DEPARTMENT OF EDUCATION AND SCIENCE (1989), *From Policy to Practice*, DES, London.

DICKINSON, W. (1993), Personal Communication.

DOMENICI, G. (1993), *Manuale Della Valutazione Scolastica*, Laterza, Bari, Italy.

DOORNBOS, K. and STEVENS, L.M. (1987), *De groei van het speciaal onderwijs: Analyse van historie onderzoek*, 's-Gravenhage, Staatsuitgeverij.

DOORNBOS, K. and STEVENS, L.M. (1988), *De groei van het speciaal onderwijs: Beeldvorming over beleid en praktijk*, 's-Gravenhage, Staatsuitgeverij.

DUNN, W. (1988), "Models of occupational therapy service provision in the school system", *American Journal of Occupational Therapy*, 42, pp. 718-723.

DUNN, W., and CAMPBELL, P.H. (1991), "Designing pediatric service provision", in W. Dunn (ed.), *Pediatric Occupational Therapy: Facilitating Effective Service Provision,* Slack, Thorofare, New Jersey, pp. 139-160.

ELLIOTT, J.L., SHIN, H., THURLOW, M.L., and YSSELDYKE, J.E. (1995), "A perspective on education and assessment in other nations: where are students with disabilities?", Synthesis Report 19, University of Minnesota, National Center on Educational Outcomes (NCO), Minneapolis, MN.

ERICKSON, R.N., THURLOW, M.L., and YSSELDYKE, J.E. (1995), *Determining Participation Rates for Students with Disabilities in Statewide Assessment Programs: the Problem with Percentages*, University of Minnesota, National Center on Educational Outcomes, Minneapolis, MN.

EVANS, J. and LUNT, I. (1994), *Markets, Competition and Vulnerability: Some Effects of Recent Legislation on Children with Special Educational Needs*, Tuffnell Press, London.

FERGUSON, D., MEYER, G., JEANCHILD, L., JUNIPER, L. and ZINGO, J. (1993), "Figuring out what to do with grownups: how teachers make inclusion 'work' for students with disabilities", *Journal of the Association for Persons with Severe Handicaps*, 17(4), pp. 218-226.

FERGUSON, D.L. (1994*a*), "Is Communication Really the Point? Some Thoughts on Interventions and Membership", *Mental Retardation*, 32(1), pp. 7-18.

FERGUSON, D.L. (1994*b*), "Magic for Teacher Work Groups: Improve Collaboration at Teacher Work Group Sessions", *Council for Exceptional Children*, 2 7(1), pp. 42-47.

FERGUSON, D.L. (in press), "Bursting Bubbles: Marrying General and Special Education Reforms", in Berres, M., Knoblock, P., Ferguson, D. L. and Woods, L. (eds.), *Restructuring Schools For All Children,* Teachers College Press, New York.

FERGUSON, D.L. (1995), "Persons with Severe Disabilities: From Mainstreaming to Supported Community Membership", in Husen, T. and Postlethwaite, T. (eds.), *The International Encyclopedia of Education*, Pergamon Press, London & New York.

FERGUSON, D.L., and MEYER, G. (in press), "Creating Together the Tools to Reinvent Schools", in Berres, M., Knoblock, P., Ferguson, D. L. and Woods, L. (eds.), *Restructuring Schools for all Children,* Teachers College Press, New York.

FERGUSON, D.L., WILLIS, C., and MEYER, G. (in press), "Widening the Stream: Ways to Think About Including 'Exceptions' in Schools", in Lehr, D. and Brown, F. (eds.), *Students with Profound Disabilities* (2nd ed.), Paul H. Brookes, Baltimore.

FERGUSON, D.L., WILLIS, C., BOLES, S., JEANCHILD, L., HOLLIDAY, L., MEYER, G., RIVERS, E., and ZITEK, M. (1993), *Regular Class Participation System* (RCPS) (Final Report Grant # H086D9001 1: US Department of Education), Specialized Training Program, University of Oregon.

FERGUSON, P.M., HIBBARD, M., LEINEN, J. and SCHAFF, S. (1990), "Supported community life: disability policy and the renewal of mediating structures", *Journal of Disability Policy*, 1, pp. 9-35.

FISH, J. and EVANS, J (1995), *Managing Special Education*, Open University Press, Milton Keynes.

FOGARTY, R. (1991), *The Mindful School: How to Integrate the Curricula*, IRI/Skylight Publishing, Inc., Palatine, Il.

FRABBONI, F. and PINTO MINERVA, F. (1994), *Manuale Di Pedagogia Generale*, Laterza, Bari, Italy.

FREY, K. (1977), *Le Teorie dei Curricula*, Feltrinelli, Milan.

FUCHS, D. and FUCHS, L. (1994), "Inclusive Schools Movement and the Radicalisation of Special Education Reform", *Exceptional Children*, 60(4), pp. 294-309.

FULLAN, M. (1991*a*), "Preface", in Porter, G.L. and Richer, D. (eds.), *op.cit.*

FULLAN, M. (1991*b*), *The New Meaning of Educational Change*, Teacher College Press, New York.

GARDNER, H. (1993), *Multiple Intelligences: the Theory in Practice*, Basic Books, New York.

GERBER, M.M. and SEMMEL, M.I. (1985), "The microeconomics of referral and reintegration: a paradigm for evaluation of special education", *Studies in Educational Evaluation*, 11, pp. 13-29.

GERRY, M. (1992), "Economic consequences of the unemployment of persons with disabilities", *Transition to Employment*, proceedings of the 1990 international symposium on the employment of persons with disabilities, Institute for the study of exceptional children and youth, University of Maryland at College Park.

GERSTEN, R., and WOODWARD, J. (1990), "Re-Thinking the Regular Education Initiative: Focus on the Classroom Teacher", *Remedial and Special Education*, 11, pp. 7-16.

GIANGRECO, M., DENNIS, R., CLONINGER, C., EDELMAN, S., and SCHATTMAN, R. (1993), "I've counted on Jon: transformational experiences of teachers educating students with disabilities", *Exceptional Children*, 59, pp. 359-372.

GIANGRECO, M.F. (1990), "Making related service decisions for students with severe handicaps: Roles, criteria, and authority", *The Journal of the Association for Persons with Severe Handicaps*, 15, pp. 22-31.

GILFOYLE, E. M., and HAYS, C. (1979), "Occupational therapy roles and functions in the education of schools with handicapped students", *American Journal of Occupational Therapy*, 33, pp. 565-576.

GIPPS, C., GROSS, H. and GOLDSTEIN, H. (1987), *Warnock's 18%: Children with Special Needs in Primary Schools*, Falmer Press, Brighton, England.

GLIEDMAN, J., and ROTH, W. (1980), *The Unexpected Minority: Handicapped Children in America*, Harcourt Brace Jovanovich, New York.

GOACHER, B., EVANS, J., WELTON, J. and WEDELL, K. (1988), *Policy and Provision for Special Educational Needs: Implementing the 1981 Act*, Cassell, London.

HACKETT, G. and PASSMORE, B. (1995), "Rankings that still rankle", *Times Educational Supplement*, November 24th, No. 4143.

HAEBERLIN, U., BLESS, G., MOSER, U. and KLAGHOFER, R. (1991*)*, *Die Integration von Lernbehinderten*, Versuche, Theorien, Enttäuschungen, Hoffnungen, Bern, Stuttgart, Wien (Haupt).

HARING, N.G., LOVITT, C., EATON, M.D., and HANSEN, C.L. (1978), *The Fourth R: Research in the Classroom,* Merrill, Ohio.

HEGARTY, S. (1989), "Modifying the school's academic organisation and teaching approaches", in Struikisma, A. J. C. and Meijer, F. (eds.), *Integration at work: the First European Community Conference on Handicap and Education*, Pedologisch Instituut, Rotterdam, pp. 92-99.

HEGARTY, S. (1993), "Reviewing the literature on integration", *European Journal of Special Needs Education*, 8, 3, pp. 194-200.

HEGARTY, S. (1994*a*), "Integration and the teacher", in Meijer, C. W.J., Pijl, S.J. and Hegarty, S. (eds.), *New Perspectives in Special Education: a Six-Country Study of Integration*, pp. 125-131, Routledge, London.

HEGARTY, S. (1994*b*), *Educating Children and Young People with Disabilities: Principles and the Review of Practices*, UNESCO, Paris.

HEGARTY, S. (1994*c*), "Integration and the Teacher", in Meijer, C.J.W., Pijl, S.J. and Hegarty, S. (eds.), *New Perspectives in Special Education: a Six Country Study of Integration,* Routledge, London, pp. 125-131.

HEHIR, T. (1993), "The Inclusive Restructured School", Manuscript prepared through the Education Development Center, Boston, MA.

HOUSER, J. (1995), "Assessing students with disabilities and limited English proficiency", Working Paper No. 95-13, US Department of Education, Office of Educational Research and Improvement, Washington, DC.

HUFFMAN, N.P. (1991), "Lesson 1: Application to practice--speech-language pathology", AOTA Self Study Series, School-based practice for related services, AOTA, Rockville, Maryland.

IRESON, J. and EVANS, P. (1995), "No easy task: structuring the curriculum for children experiencing difficulties in school", in Lunt, I., Norwich, B. and Varma, V. (eds), *Psychology and Education for Special Needs,* Ashgate Publishing, Arena.

ITALIAN DELEGATION to the OECD (1992), "Study on Integrating Students with Disabilities into Mainstream Schools", Country report, OECD, Paris.

ITALIAN DELEGATION to the OECD (1993), "Study on Integrating Students with Disabilities into Mainstream Schools", Case study report, OECD, Paris.

KYLE, J.G. (1993), "Integration of deaf children", *European Journal of Special Needs Education*, 8, 3, pp. 201-220.

LANDESMAN, S.J., and BUTTERFIELD, E.C. (1987), "Normalization and De-Institutionalization of Mentally Retarded Individuals", *American Psychologist*, 42, 8, pp. 809-816 (cited by Rispens, 1994).

LEINHARDT, G. (1992), "What Research on Learning Tells Us About Teaching", *Educational Leadership*, 49(7), pp. 20-25.

LEWIS, A. (1995), *Primary Special Needs and the National Curriculum* (2nd ed.), Routledge, London.

LIGUE INTERNATIONALE DES ASSOCIATIONS POUR LES PERSONNES HANDICAPÉES MENTALES (1990), "Education pour aider tous ceux qui ont des difficultés d'apprentissage à être membres à part entière de leurs communautés", LIAPHM, Bruxelles.

LUNDBERG, I., FROST, J. and PETERSEN, P.P. (1988), "Effects of an extensive program for stimulating phonological awareness in preschool children", *Reading Research Quaterly*, 23, pp. 263-284.

LUNT, I., EVANS, J., NORWICH, B. and WEDELL, K. (1994), *Working Together: Interschool Collaboration for Special Needs*, Fulton, London.

LYNCH, J. (1993), "Presentation at the Middle School Education Workshop", Fredericton, New Brunswick.

MARAGLIANO, R. (1988), *Didattica Scolastica: La Formazione Di Base*, Juvenilia, Bergamo, Italy.

MARAGLIANO, R. and VERTECCHI, B. (1992), *La Programmazione Didattica*, Editori Riuniti, Rome.

MCCORMICK, L., and LEE, C. (1979), "Public Law 94-142: Mandated partnerships", *American Journal of Occupational Therapy*, 33, pp. 580-589.

MCGREW, K.S., THURLOW, M.L., SHRINER, J.G. and SPIEGEL, A.N. (1992), "Inclusion of students with disabilities in national and state data collection programs", Technical Report 2, University of Minnesota, National Center on Educational Outcomes, Minneapolis, MN.

MCGREW, K.S., THURLOW, M.L. and SPIEGEL, A.N. (1993), "The Exclusion of Students with Disabilities in National and State Data Collection Programs", *Educational Evaluation and Policy Analysis*, 15 (3), pp. 339-352.

MCLAUGHLIN, M.J. (1995), "Consolidated special education funding and services: a local perspective", Policy Paper No. 5, American Institute for Research, Center for Special Education Finance (CSEF), Palo Alto, CA.

MEADOW, K. (1968), "Early Manual Communication in Relation to the Deaf Child's Intellectual, Social, and Communicative Functioning", *American Annals of the Deaf*, 113, pp. 29-41.

MEIJER, C.J.W. (1995), *Halverwege: Van Startwet Naar Streefbeeld*, Academisch Boeken Centrum.

MEIJER, C.J.W., PESCHAR, J.L. and SCHEERENS (1995), *Prikkels, De Lier,* Academisch Boeken Centrum.

MEIJER, C.J.W., PIJL, S.J. and HEGARTY, S. (eds) (1994), *New Perspectives in Special Education: a Six Country Study of Integration,* Routledge, London.

MINISTERIE VAN ONDERWIJS EN WETENSCHAPPEN (1985), *Wet op het Basisonderwijs,* 's-Gravenhage, Staatsuitgeverij.

MINISTERIE VAN ONDERWIJS EN WETENSCHAPPEN (1990), "Weer samen naar school, Perspectief om leerlingen ook in reguliere scholen onderwijs op maat te bieden", Hoofdlijnennotitie, 's-Gravenhage, SDU.

MINISTERIE VAN ONDERWIJS EN WETENSCHAPPEN (1991), *3x Akkoord,* 's-Gravenhage, SDU.

MOORES, D. (1971), *Recent Research in Manual Communication,* University of Minnesota Research, Development and Demonstration Center in Education of Handicapped Children, Occasional Paper No. 7.

MOSES, D., HEGARTY, S. and JOWETT, S. (1988), *Supporting Ordinary Schools*, NFER-Nelson, Windsor, England.

MOSHER, E.K., HASTINGS, A.H., and WAGONER, J.L. (1979), *Pursuing Equal Educational Opportunity: School Politics and the New Activists*, ERIC Clearinghouse on Urban Education, Teachers College, Columbia University, New York.

MÜLLER, H. (1989), "The 'Hamburger Schulversuch': a teaching experiment integrating the handicapped in primary schools", in Struiksma, A.J.C. and Meijer, F. (eds.), *op. cit.*

MULLINS, J. (1981), "New challenges for physical therapy in educational settings", *Physical Therapy*, 61, pp. 496-501.

NATIONAL ACADEMY OF EDUCATION (in press), *Results of Follow-up of 1994 Students Excluded from NAEP,* Stanford University, National Academy of Education, Stanford, CA.

NATIONAL ASSOCIATION OF SCHOOL BOARDS OF EDUCATION (1992), "Winners all: A call for inclusive schools", Report for the NASBE Study Group on Special Education, Alexandria, VA.

NATIONAL CENTER ON EDUCATIONAL RESTRUCTURING AND INCLUSION (1994), "National Survey on Inclusive Education", NCERI Bulletin, 1, New York.

NATIONAL CONFEDERATION FOR PARENT TEACHER ASSOCIATIONS (1996), "The state of schools report 1996", NCPTA.

NATIONAL COUNCIL FOR EDUCATIONAL TECHNOLOGY (1995), "Recording and reporting under the Code of Practice", NCET, London.

NATIONAL CURRICULUM COUNCIL (1989), "Curriculum guidance no. 2: a curriculum for all", NCC, York.

NATIONAL EDUCATION ASSOCIATION (1992), "Resolution B-20, Education for all students with disabilities", Washington, DC.

NATIONAL FOUNDATION FOR EDUCATIONAL RESEARCH (1992), "OECD/CERI project: Integration in the school: reports of the case studies undertaken in the UK", NFER, Slough.

NIEDERMANN, A., BLESS, G. and SASSENROTH, M. (1992), *Heilpädagogischer Stützunterricht*. Ergebnisse einer Meinungsumfrage in Deutschfreiburg, Aspekte 44, Luzern (Edition SZH).

NODDINGS, N. (1993), "Excellence as a Guide to Educational Conversation", *Teachers' College Record*, 94(4), pp. 730-743.

NODDINGS, N. (1993), *The Challenge to Care in Schools: an Alternative Approach to Education*, Teachers College Press, New York.

NORDAHL, T. and OVERLAND, T. (1993), *Participation or Social Isolation*, KUF, Oslo.

NORRIS, J.A. and HOFFMAN, P.R. (1990), "Language intervention within naturalistic environments", *Language Speech, and Hearing Services in the Schools*, 21, pp. 72-84.

O'BRIEN, M.A. and O'LEARY, T. (1988), "Evolving to the classroom model: Speech-language service for the mentally retarded", Seminars in Speech and Language, 9, pp. 355-366.

O'HANLON, C. (1993), *Special Education Integration in Europe*, Fulton, London.

O'NEIL, J. (1994), "Can inclusion work? A conversation with Jim Kauffinan and Mara Sapon-Shevin", *Educational Leadership*, 52(4), pp. 7-11.

OAKES, J., and LIPTON, M. (1992), "De-Tracking Schools: Early Lessons from the Field", *Phi Delta Kappan*, 73(6), pp. 448-454.

OECD (1992), "Employment Policies for People with Disabilities", Labour market and social policy occasional papers No. 8, Paris.

OECD (1994), *The Integration of Disabled Children into Mainstream Education: Ambitions, Theories and Practices*, Paris.

OECD (1995), *Integrating Students with Special Needs into Mainstream Schools*, Paris.

OECD (1995a), *Our Children at Risk*, Paris.

OFFICE FOR STANDARDS IN EDUCATION (OFSTED) (1996), *Promoting High Achievement for Pupils with Special Educational Needs in Mainstream Schools*, HMSO, London.

OFFICE OF TECHNOLOGY ASSESSMENT (1992), "Testing in American schools: asking the right questions", Office of Technology Assessment, Washington, DC.

OTTENBACHER, K.J (1991), "Conflicting views: Who knows best?", AOTA Self Study Series: School-based practice for related services, Rockville.

PARRISH, T.B. (1994), "Fiscal issues in special education: removing incentives for restrictive placements" (Policy Paper No. 4), American Institutes for Research, Center for Special Education Finance (CSEF), Palo Alto, CA.

PERNER, D. (1991), "Leading the Way: the Role of School Administrators in Integration", in Porter, G. L. and Richler, D. (eds.), *op. cit.*

PERNER, D. (1993), "All students attend regular classes in neighbourhood schools: a case study of three schools in Woodstock, New Brunswick, Canada", Report for the OECD/CERI 'Active Life for Disabled Youth -- Integration in the School' project, OECD, Paris.

PERNER, D. and PORTER, G.L. (1996), "Creating inclusive schools: changing roles and strategies", in Hilton, A. and Ringlaben, R. (eds.), *Best and Promising Practices in Developmental Disabilities*, Pro-Ed Inc., Austin, Tx.

PERNER, D. and STONE, J.A. (in press), *Multi-Level Instruction: a Curricular Approach for Inclusion*.

PIJL, S.J. and MEIJER, C.J.W. (1991), "Does Integration Count for much? An Analysis of the Practices of Integration in Eight Countries", *European Journal of Special Needs Education*, 6, pp. 100-111.

PIJL, S.J. and MEIJER, C.W.J. (1994), "Analysis of the findings", in Meijer, C.W.J., Pijl, S.J.and Hegarty, S. (eds.), *op. cit.,* pp. 132-140.

PORSTEINSSON, T. (1995), "Special Pedagogy", unpublished paper.

PORTER, G.L. (1986), "School Integration in Districts 28 & 29", *Education New Brunswick*, New Brunswick Department of Education, Fredericton. Reprinted in Forest, M. (ed.) (1987), *More Education Integration,* G. Allan Roeher Institute, Toronto, Ont.

PORTER, G.L. (1991), "The Method and Resource Teacher: a Collaborative Consultant Model", in Porter, G. L. and Richler, D. (eds.), *op. cit.*

PORTER, G.L. (1995), "Organization of Schooling: Achieving Access and Quality Through Inclusion", *Prospects: Quarterly Review of Comparative Education,* Vol. XXV, No. 2, UNESCO, Paris, pp. 299-309.

PORTER, G.L. and RICHLER, D. (1990), "Changing special education practice: law, advocacy and innovation", *Canadian Journal of Community Mental Health,* Vol. 9, No. 2, pp. 65-78.

PORTER, G.L., WILSON, M., KELLY, B. and van OTTER, J. (1991), "Problem Solving Teams: a Thirty-Minute Peer-Helping Model", in Porter, G. L. and Richler, D. (eds.), *op. cit.*

PROVINCE OF NEW BRUNSWICK (1988), "Working guidelines on integration", Student Services Branch, New Brunswick Department of Education, Fredericton.

PROVINCE OF NEW BRUNSWICK (1994), "Best practices for inclusion", Student Services Branch, New Brunswick Department of Education, Fredericton.

QUIGLEY, S. and FRISINA, D. (1961), *Institutionalization and Psycho-Educational Development of Deaf Children,* Council for Exceptional Children, Washington DC.

RAINFORTH, B., and YORK, J. (1987), "Integrating related services in community instruction", *Journal of the Association for the Severely Handicapped,* 6, pp. 248-252.

REYNOLDS, D. (1991), "Changing Ineffective Schools", in Ainscow, M. (ed.), *op. cit.,* pp. 92-105.

RISPENS, J. (1994), "Re-Thinking the Course of Integration: What Can we Learn from the Past?", in Meijer, C.W.J., Pijl, S.J. and Hegarty, S. (eds.), *op. cit.,* pp. 113-124.

ROYEEN, C.B., and COUTINHO, M. (1991), "The special education administrator's perspective", in Dunn W. (ed.), *Pediatric occupational therapy: Facilitating effective service Provision,* Slack, Thorofare, New Jersey.

SAGE, D. (1989), "Obstacles to implementing school integration", Paper presented at the conference of the Council for Exceptional Children, San Francisco.

SAMMONS, P., THOMAS, S., MORTIMORE, P., OWEN, C. and PENNELL, H. (1994), *Assessing School Effectiveness,* University of London Institute of Education.

SAULLE, M.R. (1994), "Legislation Issues", Paper presented at the world conference on special educational needs: access and quality, 7-10 June, Salamanca, Spain (cited by Meijer, 1995).

SCHULZ, J. and TURNBULL, A. (1984), *Mainstreaming Handicapped Students: a Guide for Classroom Teachers,* Allyn and Bacon, Boston.

SCHWEIZERISCHE KONFERENZ DER KANTONALEN ERZIEHUNGSDIREKTOREN (EDK) (1995), *Empfehlungen und Beschlüsse,* Dossier 36A, Bern.

SIZER, T. (1992), *Horace's School: Re-Designing the American School,* Houghton Mifflin, Boston.

SKRTIC, T. (1991), "The special education paradox: equity as the way to excellence", *Harvard Educational Review,* 61(2), pp. 148-206.

SKRTIC, T.M. (1991), *Behind Special Education: a Critical Analysis of Professional Culture and School Organization,* Love Publishing, Denver.

SLAVIN, R.E. (1987), "A theory of school and classroom organisation", *Educational Psychologist,* 22 (2), pp. 89-108.

SLOAN, L.J., ALBERG, J., DENNY, K., HASAZI, S., MCLAUGHLIN, M., and REPP, A.C. (1992), "Integration in the schools: Practices in the United States", report submitted to the OECD Study on Integrating Students with Disabilities into Mainstream Schools.

SLOAN, L.J., DENNY, R.K., and REPP, A.C. (1992), "Integration practices in the United States: A composite case study", report submitted to the OECD Study on Integrating Students with Disabilities into Mainstream Schools.

SMULL, M., and BELLAMY, G. (1991), "Community Services for Adults with Disabilities: Policy Challenges in the Emerging Support Paradigm", in Meijer, L., Peck, C. and Brown, L. (eds.), *Critical Issues in the Lives of People with Severe Disabilities*, Paul H. Brookes, Baltimore, Md.

SPARLING, J.W. (1980), "The transdisciplinary approach with the developmentally delayed child", *Physical and Occupational Therapy in Pediatrics*, 1, pp. 3-11.

STEVENSON, E. (1964), "A Study of the Educational Achievement of Deaf Children of Deaf Parents", *California News,* 80, p. 143.

STUCKLESS, R. and BIRCH, J. (1964), "The Influence of Early Communication on the Linguistic Development of Deaf Children", *American Annals of the Deaf*, 111, pp. 452-460 and 499-504.

SULLIVAN, T. J. (1995), *Sociology: Concepts and Applications in a Diverse World*, 3rd ed., Allyn and Bacon, Boston.

THE AMERICAN OCCUPATIONAL THERAPY ASSOCIATION (1987), *Guidelines for Occupational Therapy Services in School Systems*, AOTA, Rockville, Maryland.

THE AMERICAN PHYSICAL THERAPY ASSOCIATION (1985), *Physical Therapy Practice in Educational Environments: Policies, Guidelines, and Background Information,* APTA, Washington, DC.

THURLOW, M.L., SCOTT, D.L., and YSSELDYKE, J.E. (1995), *A Compilation of States' Guidelines for Including Students with Disabilities in Assessments*, University of Minnesota, National Center on Educational Outcomes, Minneapolis, MN.

TIBERI, S. (1991), "Analisi dei casi e delle situazioni nell'esperienza didattica", in De Anna, L. (ed.), *La Scuola e i Disabili*, L'ed., Rome.

TIMES EDUCATIONAL SUPPLEMENT (1995), Report No. 4114, p. 1, May 5th.

TRISCIUZZI, L. (1993), *Manuale Di Didattica Per L'handicap*, Laterza, Bari, Italy.

US DEPARTMENT OF EDUCATION (1994), "Sixteenth annual report to Congress on the implementation of the Individuals with Disabilities Education Act", US Department of Education, Washington, DC.

US SENATE, COMMITTEE ON LABOR AND PUBLIC WELFARE, SUBCOMMITTEE ON THE HANDICAPPED (1976), "Education of the Handicapped Act as amended through December 31, 1975", Report No. 72-611, US Government Printing Office, Washington, DC.

UNESCO (1994), "The Salamanca Statement and Framework for Action on Special Needs Education", World conference on special needs education, Salamanca, UNESCO, Paris.

UNESCO (1995), *Access and Quality*, final report of the World conference on Special Needs Education, OECD, Paris (also published by the Ministry of Education and Science, Madrid, 1995).

UNITED STATES DEPARTMENT OF EDUCATION (1992), "Fourteenth Annual Report to Congress", Washington, DC.

VERNON, M. and KOH, S. (1972), "Effects of oral preschool communication compared to manual communication on education and communication in deaf children", in Mindel, E. and Vernon, M. (eds), *They grow in silence*, National Association of the Deaf, Silver Spring, Md.

VERSTEGEN, D.A. (1994), "Fiscal provisions of the Individuals with Disabilities Education Act: Historical Overview" (Policy Paper No. 2), American Institutes for Research, Center for Special Education Finance (CSEF), Palo Alto, CA.

VERSTEGEN, D.A. (1995), "Consolidated special education funding and services: a federal perspective" (Policy Paper No. 6), American Institutes for Research, Center for Special Education Finance (CSEF), Palo Alto, CA.

WAGNER, M., NEWMAN, L., D'AMICO, R., JAY, E.D., BUTLER-NALIN, N., MARDER, C., and COX, R. (1991), "Youth with disabilities: How are they doing?", first comprehensive report from the national longitudinal transition study of special education students, SRI International, Menlo Park, California.

WALBERG, H.J. (1993), "Learning 'disabilities' revisited", *European Journal of Special Needs Education*, 8, 3, pp. 289-302.

WEDELL, K. (1993), "Special education: the next 25 years in: National Commission on Education", Briefings, Heinemann, London.

WEDELL, K. (1995), "Making Inclusive Education Ordinary", *British Journal of Special Education*, 22 (3), pp. 100-104.

WEDELL, K. (1995), *Putting the Code of Practice into Practice: Meeting Special Educational Needs in the School and Classroom*, University of London Institute of Education.

WIGGENS, G. (1989), "The Futility of Trying to Teacher Everything Important", *Educational Leadership*, 47 (3), pp. 57-59.

WILL, M.C. (1986), "Educating children with learning problems: A shared responsibility", *Exceptional Children*, 51, pp. 411-416.

WILLIAMS, P. (1993), "Integration of students with moderate learning difficulties", *European Journal of Special Needs Education*, 8, 3, pp. 303-319.

YORK, J., RAINFORTH, B., and GIANGRECO, M.F. (1990), "Transdisciplinary teamwork and integrated therapy: Clarifying the misconceptions", *Pediatric Physical Therapy*, 12, pp. 107-110.

YSSELDYKE, J.E., THURLOW, M.L., MCGREW, K.S. and SHRINER, J.G. (1994), *Recommendations for Making Decisions about the Participation of Students with Disabilities in Statewide Assessment Programs*, University of Minnesota, National Center on Educational Outcomes, Minneapolis, MN.

YSSELDYKE, J.E., THURLOW, M.L., MCGREW, K.S. and VANDERWOOD, M. (1994), "Making decisions about the inclusion of students with disabilities in large-scale assessments", Synthesis Report 13, University of Minnesota, National Center on Educational Outcomes, Minneapolis, MN.

OECD PUBLICATIONS, 2, rue André-Pascal, 75775 PARIS CEDEX 16
PRINTED IN FRANCE
(96 97 03 1 P) ISBN 92-64-15589-9 – No. 49655 1998